# MOMENTS
## RIGHTLY PLACED
### An Aleutian Memoir

Written and Illustrated by **Ray Hudson**

With a Foreword by Gary Snyder

EPICENTER PRESS

FAIRBANKS · SEATTLE

Front cover and title page: Anfesia Shapsnikoff during one of the classes she taught in 1971 at the Baranov Museum in Kodiak, Alaska. Photo by Roger Page, courtesy of the Kodiak Historical Society. Back cover: Anfesia Shapsnikoff transplanting wild garlic in 1972. Photo by Ray Hudson.

Epicenter Press, Inc., is a regional press founded in Alaska whose interests include but are not limited to the arts, history, environment, and diverse cultures and lifestyles of the North Pacific and high latitudes. We seek both the traditional and innovative in publishing nonfiction tradebooks, contemporary art and photography giftbooks, and destination travel guides emphasizing Alaska, Washington, Oregon, and California.

Text and illustrations © 1998 by Ray Hudson. Original woodcut prints were produced in sumi ink on sheng shuen (dan) paper.

Editor: Tricia Brown
Illustrations: Ray Hudson
Mapmaker: Debra Dubac
Proofreader: Lois Kelly
Cover and text design, typesetting: Elizabeth Watson
Printer: Transcontinental Printing

Library of Congress Catalog Card Number: 97-078444

ISBN 0-945397-49-6

To order single copies of *Moments Rightly Placed*, mail $14.95 (Washington residents add $1.29 sales tax) plus $5 for first-class mailing to: Epicenter Press, Box 82368, Kenmore, WA 98028.

Booksellers: Retail discounts are available from our distributor, Graphic Arts Center Publishing, Box 10306, Portland, OR 97210. Phone 800-452-3032.

Printed in Canada

First printing April 1998

10 9 8 7 6 5 4 3 2 1

# Acknowledgments

*Okalena Lekanoff-Gregory gathers grass near the head of Unalaska Lake in August 1984.*
PHOTO BY MARTI MURRAY.

I want to thank friends at Unalaska who read and commented on an earlier draft of this work: Sophie Sherebernikoff, Gert and Sam Svarny, and the late Platonida Gromoff. Because of them I have been able to correct some errors of fact and emphasis. Of course, those friends are not responsible for the final shape or content of this book, nor for the remaining errors.

I am very grateful for the suggestions given by Dorothy Jones, Kent Sturgis, Tricia Brown, Valerie Griffith, Lydia Black, and Cate Goethals. I am indebted to Anne E. Depue for her careful readings, her astute suggestions, and advice.

Thanks also to Wendy A. Svarny-Hawthorne, Shareholder Affairs, Ounalashka Corporation; Jack and Marti Murray; Okalena Lekanoff-Gregory; Suzi Dengler Golodoff; Unalaska City School; the Kodiak Historical Society; and Vincent M. and Doretta Tutiakoff.

I want to give special thanks to my wife, Shelly, with whom I shared twenty wonderful years in the Aleutians. Finally, I want to dedicate this book to my mother with love, gratitude, and enduring admiration.

# Contents

*Ray Hudson with James David Gregory and basket grass on Amaknak Island.*
PHOTO BY MARTI MURRAY.

# Foreword

Walking the hills, teaching school, learning basket-weaving, sitting down to tea with the neighbors—Ray Hudson's memoir is a pearl of real life insight, unencumbered by theory or ecstasy. The chilly damp windy Aleutian Chain, and its proud, reticent Orthodox Christian Native people would not usually be a first choice of habitat for a twenty-two-year-old just out of college. Ray went to teach for a year and stayed for many. It seems he was first enchanted by walking the wide green hills, and next by the beauty of traditional Aleut grass baskets.

This remarkable, fresh book is an understated manual for how to learn a place, how to connect with the old-timers, how to wait 'til deemed ready, and how to undertake a practice that will invisibly transform you.

It is rich in vivid, subtle, and original writing strategies. Ray was lucky and patient enough to get to know Anfesia Shapsnikoff, a woman of considerable strength and knowledge who became his basket and language teacher; and (among many others) Henry Swanson with his tales of fishing, trapping, handling small boats in outrageous waters, and of the nuttiness of World War II at that far end of the world.

There are poems in Ray's writing, as in the details of twining and twisting the weft and warp of baskets. A rich life flourishes behind Scrabble games in the dark winter; today's gossip and nineteenth-century tales meet over tea, seal meat, and fish pie. He tells of the town meetings and the patient struggles with new economics and insensitive bureaucracies; and the risk of losing it all.

What we need to know about the fit between place and culture, about "real human beings" in a way, is all here. This book is a lovely, tightly woven little basket in its own right.

—Gary Snyder

RUSSIA

Fox Islands

Nikolski
Inanudak Bay
Okmos Volcano
Chernofski
Kashega
Makushin
Makushin Volcano
Unalaska
Beaver Inlet
Biorka
Akutan Island

Umnak Island

Unalaska Island

Attu
Near Islands
Kiska
Rat Islands
Andreanof Islands
Atka
Fox Islands

Pribilof Islands

Bering Sea

Aleutian Is

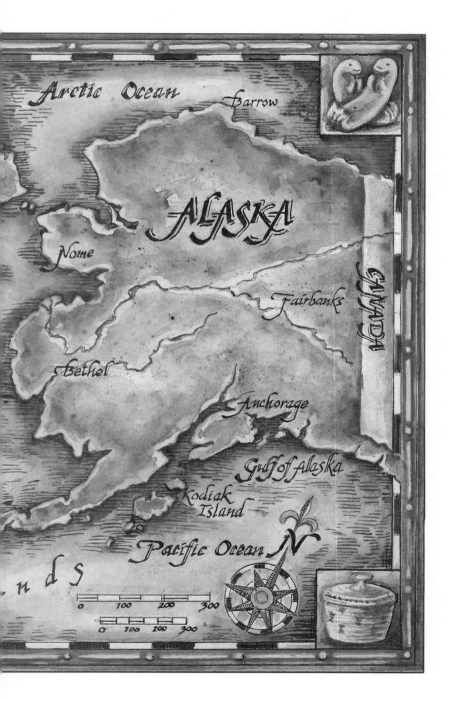

*An unfinished basket bottom by Anfesia Shapsnikoff among blades of wild rye.*
PHOTO BY MARTI MURRAY, VINCENT M. TUTIAKOFF SR. COLLECTION.

# Author's Note

*Ray Hudson sketching with Nugget at Agamgik Bay.*
PHOTO BY SHELLY HUDSON.

In 1964, I arrived at Unalaska, a village of about three hundred people in the Eastern Aleutian Islands. Eventually I began a study of Aleut basketry with Sophie Pletnikoff, a remarkable self-taught weaver, and with Anfesia Shapsnikoff, a classical Attu weaver. Aleut basketry is among the finest grass-weaving in the world. As Sophie Pletnikoff made abundantly clear, Aleut weaving is not a stagnant art but one which, drawing on thousands of years of tradition, continues to refine techniques, to incorporate new designs, to reflect circumstances of the times.

During the years I studied with Sophie and Anfesia, I met many remarkable people at Unalaska, Nikolski, and Akutan—the three surviving villages in the Eastern Aleutians. They taught me so much. This book chronicles some of the circumstances of those years and attempts to explain some of the things I learned while learning to weave a basket.

This is a memoir and not a scholarly work. It is a series of impressions and reflections on a place of profound beauty and on a people who are indeed, as Philemon Tutiakoff frequently said they were, "the best people on earth." A few reference notes have been provided for those interested in investigating subjects in greater depth.

# 1

# An Autumn Hike

The breeze began at my back as I followed the dirt road running flawlessly eastward through the village. It wove among scattered clusters of houses and sheds, wind-blasted and continually patched. It pushed the knapsack holding my lunch and poncho, and teased the late September buttercups bobbing like buoys over high grass. As soon as the road edged the lake, the breeze veered sideways and rustled the iridescence on a couple of harlequins. It momentarily settled among the abandoned Quonset huts, cabanas, barracks, and warehouses whose veined gray wood and empty windows overshadowed the lake for the next half-mile.

After holding to the circumference of the valley floor for another quarter-mile, the road buckled up a moderate grade into a congregation of treeless hills. The breeze was out front to greet me as I started climbing. Even if this wind couldn't decide where it was going, I knew where I was headed: to Ugadaga, the most accessible of the bays of Unalaska Island's Beaver Inlet. Just as there are no trees in the

Aleutian Islands, so there are no beavers. The Russian word for otter was the same as that for beaver, and thus the Inlet of Sea Otters had become Beaver Inlet.

Where the road began climbing, a wooden tower stood in ruined guard over a World War II prisoner-of-war camp. Now nothing but tangled barbed wire and two sunken wooden huts, the stockade had been built after direct hostilities with the forces of Japan were over and consequently had held only drunk and disorderly American GIs.

Heavily eroded by an errant creek adopting the road for part of its course, the way climbed steeply through another military ghost town perched on the slopes below Raven's Roost. In a few minutes, restored to packed earth, the road cornered a ridge and sloped into a valley on the side of a hill overlooking the world. This high, open bowl, in winter as smooth as the inside of a broken eggshell, was always a place of pure protected contemplation, more so when filled with lush green summer foliage or autumn's anchored yellow ferns and grass.

In succeeding years, whenever I hiked to Ugadaga and got this far, I felt I had come far enough, that nothing could be more beautiful. Nothing ever was, yet I almost never stopped but continued up an incline until the road veered left toward the summit. At this corner the trail down to Ugadaga Bay began at an alpine pond where a few iron rod posts, once supports for an encircling barbed wire fence, kept their skeletal guard. Each twisted like a line of cursive *e*'s climaxing with a sharpened point, the posts rusted at angles, forever off-duty.

The iron posts, the prisoner-of-war camp, the wind-whitened cabanas—all were remnants of World War II. Beginning in 1940, military crews and civilian workers had irrevocably altered Unalaska Island by June 3 and 4, 1942, when it was attacked by Japanese planes from the carriers *Ryujo* and *Junyo*. Following the raids, the army and navy had continued bulldozing and building until the base at Dutch Harbor/Unalaska had accommodated 60,000 people.

Angling, jackknifing, and switchbacking across the fragile subarctic hills, roads veined the valleys fanning out of coves and bays near the central harbor. Double-storied barracks, two-room cabanas, cement-floored latrines, warehouses, mess halls, offices, and Quonset huts; exercise fields, ammunition dumps, wooden walkways to escape the mud. After twenty years, abandonment had washed away dirt and fine gravel, and most roads remained passable. In a few places culverts had been flushed out and wooden bridges were weakening. Sea cliffs had reclaimed a few presumptuous roads along the shore. Salt air and wind and rains had stripped paint from wooden buildings and bleached the excellent lumber to dark gray in the rain and to silver in moonlight. Storms had ripped camouflaging from metal Quonset huts and incessant mist had rusted them to shades of orange and brown.

By 1964 only the more remote buildings and Quonsets had any windows left. Sinks, toilets, showers, anything that had made the structures livable, were gone—victims of vandalism; but how could it be vandalism when there were hundreds and hundreds of deserted buildings and so few kids with rocks? Victims of deliriously overjoyed units departing "back to the States"; victims of fishing crews who loaded their boats with whatever they could literally rip off and headed for Seattle. A salvaging contractor in the early 1950s had chainsawed the power and telephone poles to more easily recover copper wire. Then twenty years of Aleutian weather had rotted steps, buckled floors, blown off doors or pitched them sideways, twisted on a single recalcitrant hinge.

These derelict buildings always slowed my hikes. I hoped I'd chance upon some relic of the war, but rust and rats and picnickers had long since reduced buildings to empty shells. But how convenient they were in the rain! How comforting to get out of heavy mist for a few minutes, to squat at the doorway or perch on a windowsill as light, filtered by clouds or gospel clean, moved with the wind.

The alpine pond was surrounded by a dense growth of greenery: grasses, cushioned mossberry bushes, clusters of late blossoms. I sat on a lichen-darkened rock, munched at a candy bar, and saw no evidence of that wind which alters the world. The Aleutian Islands brace themselves along the southern perimeter of the Bering Sea in a grand arc a thousand miles long. Caught in crossfire between cold and warm air circulating above the Bering Sea and the North Pacific Ocean, the islands are continually sculpted by winds of exceptional velocity and persistence, giving credence to a line in the *Coast Pilot*, that indispensable guide for mariners: "No other area in the world is recognized as having worse weather in general than that which the Aleutian Islands experience."

Sixty miles south, the Aleutian trench plummets to a depth between 2,400 and 4,000 fathoms. With more than forty-five volcanoes, the chain is a long seismic nerve. The region itself is defined by Aleut settlements; and three weeks earlier I had arrived at Unalaska, the largest community in the Eastern Aleutians, as one of three new schoolteachers on a staff of four. Already I had heard Unalaska Island referred to as "the rock," as "the end of the world." However, it was clear that when viewed in the context of the entire Aleutian Chain, Unalaska was near the beginning. Perhaps, some might say, the beginning of the end. Starting on the Alaska Peninsula at 160° W, near Kupreanof Point, the Aleutian region extends past the 180° meridian to just beyond 173° E. The two ends of the arc lie at about 55° N latitude dipping at their center to approximately 51° N, within brushing range of the warmer Japanese current.

In the eighteenth century, the Chain was named after Catherine the Great: Catherine's Archipelago. Although this name did not stick, the Russian subdivision of the islands remained. Closest to Russia are the Near Islands, the largest of which is Attu. East some two hundred miles are the Rat Islands, the best known of which are Kiska and Amchitka. The minuscule Delarof Islands are abreast the bulkier Andreanof Islands in the Central Aleutians. Adak and Atka are the most prominent of the Andreanofs.

Atka lies some five hundred miles east of Attu and a hundred miles farther east are a cluster of volcanoes known as the Islands of Four Mountains. The Fox Islands, including Umnak, Unalaska, and Akutan Islands, begin the Eastern Aleutians. The largest of the Fox Islands, Unimak, nearly brushes the tip of the Alaska Peninsula off of which a number of small island groups concludes the Aleutian region.

Since the early nineteenth century, permanent Aleut settlements in the Pribilof Islands north of the Fox Islands have brought those islands into the cultural, political, and economic life of the area.

The island on which I had arrived is approximately eighty-five miles long and thirty-nine miles wide, with an area of about twelve hundred square miles. Unalaska is the second largest of the Aleutian Islands, but its fifty-one bays and innumerable coves produce the longest perimeter of any of the islands. Located between latitudes 53° 15' and 54° N and between longitudes 166° and 168° W, Unalaska follows the general curve of this segment of the Aleutian Arc (about North 60° E).

Two bay complexes nearly bisect the island: seventeen-mile-long Beaver Inlet splits the eastern end of the island, while Makushin Bay reaches more than ten miles from the northwest toward the head of Beaver Inlet. North of Makushin Bay is the island's highest peak, the 6,680-foot Makushin Volcano.

Below the eastern slopes of Makushin, a vast intricate harbor opens onto the Bering Sea. This is Unalaska Bay, composed of seven individual bays among which are the most protected anchorages in the Aleutian Islands. The wide expanse from Eider Point to Priest Rock is bisected by irregular Amaknak Island, which provides a superb harbor and shelters the nearby shores of Unalaska Island.

The harbor on Amaknak, *Uda x̂tan* in Aleut but renamed "Dutch Harbor" by eighteenth-century Russians, was so welcomed by mariners that its name frequently usurped Unalaska as the name for the community. Local folks naturally resented this. After an airstrip was located off this harbor, arriving transients frequently said they'd flown into Dutch Harbor. Locals would smile a little and comment, "I hope you were wearing a life preserver."

A stone's throw from Amaknak Island, a shallow creek empties from a lake creating a narrow peninsula along the southeastern shore of Unalaska Island. Here the village of Unalaska sits like a beached fisherman scanning the bay before him for incoming ships. Immediately east of the village, Mount Newhall blocks the morning sun and begins a ridge of shoreline mountains that lead northeast to Summer Bay.

By mid-September this bay had already become one of my favorite destinations because, unlike the rocky beach in town, its sandy shores were kind to stray glass floats and other temporary treasures. There were always driftwood branches or cast up fish boxes available for fire, and the water running from the nearby lake was fresh unless the tide was coming in. If it rained, the heavy-duty Quonset huts—elephant huts—along the lake shore provided shelter.

A dirt road to Summer Bay had been scratched at the base of the ridge during World War II, but the year I arrived it was covered by a dozen rock slides, some fresh, some shouldering growths of lupine and salmonberry bushes. The slides now accommodated a trail, and, although I knew they were continually slipping on themselves in a slow motion plunge into the Bering Sea, I also figured they wouldn't mind me scampering across. Traversing the raw stones of a new slide was like wading a fresh wound.

On this late September day, however, I had decided to be a bit more adventurous and hike inland. My neighbor, Polly Lekanoff, had cautioned me about going out alone, but what was the alternative? Now I sat near the crest of a green wave. Higher up the vegetation became sparse; the rocky slopes, precipitous.

The higher elevations of the north end of Unalaska Island, like many of the other fifteen major islands, show complex configurations of teethed summits, gnarled ridges with precipitous ravines, rock walls thrust upwards overshadowing glacial lakes, everywhere intersected by valleys. Everywhere ice, water, and wind devour what was made by fire. And higher still, above the multitude of ancient eroded peaks, rise the deceptively placid slopes of more recent volcanoes.

Below the volcanoes, below the ragged summits, muscled slopes relax toward the coast. Southern portions of these larger islands (and often entire smaller islands) have rippled from the sea like elevated plateaus. Across the Aleutians, shores unfold with rounded grassy bluffs, broken grass-capped pinnacles, eroded cliffs laced with waterfalls, sea caves palming the crested tide, rock ledges crowded with crustaceans, and great boulder-strewn beaches. The precipitous coasts occasionally open to stretches of finer rock or sand, into protected bays coveted by mariners.

As I stood ready to descend the trail to Ugadaga, I looked back down the long slopes, across the valley and lake, beyond the village, over Amaknak Island, above the far reaches of the bay, where the crushed dome of Makushin rose in the west. As with other domed

Alaskan volcanoes there is a paradoxical symmetry about Makushin:
Its roots of fire are mirrored, in the words of the geologist Harald
Drewes, by a "glacier with tongues." In 1910 Isidor Solovyov, the great
Aleut storyteller, told about the transformation and renewal of
Kamgiligan, the Spirit of Makushin Volcano. It is a tale of a god who
became human, not to redeem the world but for his own fulfillment.
Kamgiligan wanted a human wife and annoyed his companion spirits
until they gave him permission to leave the volcano. He could marry
only by becoming a man. He could become a man only by being born
to a married woman.

> When the world of water was map flat with sudden calm, a breath
> exhaled and final, he knew his desire. No married woman caught his
> eye, but he saw a virgin about to drink from a stream. Transforming
> himself into dust he settled on the water. A particle of god, earth stung
> with fire, entered her. As her pregnancy became visible, the virgin's mind
> darkened; and, resorting to violence, she bore the child early and buried
> it under a piece of sod. The Spirit wept with disappointment, then left
> his grave and stepped into fire. Shadows of flame and sulfur
> surrounded him with healing.
>
> Soon he was talking once more about living among Aleuts and his
> companions said, "You're not doing that again, are you?"
>
> "No, I'm not doing that again."
>
> "Well, go! But get inside a married woman. If you repeat what you
> did before you'll be completely smashed apart and burnt in fire."
>
> Kamgiligan was incorrigible and went looking for a virgin. As luck
> would have it, a married woman was about to drink water as he went by.
> Turning into dust, he entered her and in time she gave birth to a child.
> He grew up, married a young woman, and they themselves had a child.
>
> His father-in-law worried that Kamgiligan lacked hunting skills so
> he took time to give him lessons. Now, as the Spirit of Makushin waited,
> he thought about his wife. He thought of her by lamplight at the sea's
> edge, by starlight when the wave crested: wife of fire, tent of flame, who
> knew nothing about volcanoes or the glory of her husband who was, at
> best, an indifferent hunter. He smiled to himself.
>
> Her father had given him a spear and instructed him in whale

*hunting. Well, he had tried. As much as he disliked the rapt insatiable*
*sea in the eyelid-thin boat, as the bulk of the whale darkened his view*
*he had thrust his spear into blackness.*

*Now he must wait, uneating, unsleeping. If the dead whale floated*
*his wife's village would hold him in honor. And, if not, he had been human*
*awhile, had laughed immoderately, had tasted the relish of winter's*
*deprivations, had held his wife and seen the eye of her mind ignite.*

*He thought of her by lamplight at the sea's edge, by starlight as the*
*wave crested and the body of the whale rose like a dark tongue.*

I had no hopes for transformation myself when the DC-3 landed
at Dutch Harbor in August 1964. Twenty-two years old, with a bache-
lor's in philosophy, the result of a mediocre pursuit of learning that
had centered around Hume and the positivists, with memorable
classes on Milton and the Restoration poets taught by David Wagoner
and "Types of Contemporary Poetry" taught by Theodore Roethke, I
stepped off the plane to teach first and second grades to twelve Aleut
children. I had absolutely no idea what I was doing. My liberal arts
degree had assured a delayed ending to an extended adolescence.

I felt a sweet irrational victory over my father, whose life of measured practicality could not comprehend the usefulness of a degree
in philosophy. He was such a masterful mechanic I swear he could lay
his hands on a piece of broken machinery and divine its problems.
That he could not divine what moved his son, that I took so many
years to value his skills and temperament, was common in relationships between fathers and sons.

Only once had the reticence that encased both of us broken.
With raised voices he had demanded I take classes that would help
me earn a living and I had unfairly accused him of thinking only
about money. We both looked forward to my first paycheck.

After high school I had lived at home during two years at a community college and in a dorm for the first year at the University of
Washington. My cousin Neal and I shared an apartment for my senior
year. Coming to Unalaska, living in an apartment the school board
had reserved, I would be on my own for the first time in my life. The
fact that the Unalaska School Board had difficulty filling their four

teaching positions and were willing to hire anyone with a degree in anything would give me, I thought, one or two years to decide where I wanted my life to go.

The trip from Seattle had been my first plane flight, and the farther I flew, the smaller the planes became until the Reeve Aleutian Airways DC-6 from Anchorage to Cold Bay, at the tip of the Alaska Peninsula, shrank to a DC-3 for the final leg of the journey. If I'd known their record for safety and long service, I'd have been less nervous about the exposed wires, the shattering vibrations, the shafts of wind that seeped through the plane's walls.

I sat next to Hilda Berikoff, who did little to reassure me. But then, I thought, if this old woman isn't panicking, I guess I shouldn't either. She grilled me with consummate mastery, appraised my shortcomings with deft skill and courtesy, and shrugged as though saying, "Don't expect to be liked. You're here to teach."

Years later I was talking with Hilda at one of the senior luncheons. She had become the town's eldest resident.

"How long have you been here now?" she asked.

"Twenty-eight years, Hilda."

"Seems like fifty," she replied.

Sometimes it seemed like fifty to me, so much had changed. I would eventually teach at Unalaska for twenty-five years, spend two years in the army and one year back at college. The town would burgeon from a village of three hundred people, primarily Aleut, to a community where over four thousand immigrants jettisoned their lives to produce one of the busiest and most profitable fishing ports in the United States. The Aleut community would remain the island's anchor, the permanent expression of life in the Aleutians.

This book covers the years 1964 to 1973. These were years that saw the king crab boom and the initiation of organized participation by Aleuts in the development of their land under the Alaska Native Claims Settlement Act. These were the years I knew Anfesia Shapsnikoff, a woman who would sign many of the letters she wrote to me *Unangam ilan uchiitilan*, your Aleut teacher.

Anfesia had lived at Unalaska since 1905, having moved with her mother from the village of Atka in the Central Aleutians. Her father had been from Atka while her mother had been born at Attu, the most western of the Aleutians. With varying degrees of mastery but with enough facility to converse, Anfesia spoke the Atkan, Attuan, and Unalaskan dialects of Aleut. She was literate in Aleut, Russian, and English. A champion of Aleut culture, she had represented the Aleutians on behalf of the territory and, after 1959, the state of Alaska on several occasions.

To be accurate, I wasn't formally introduced to Anfesia Shapsnikoff until I had been in the village for over a year and had experienced the island's four seasons: the prolonged autumn or berry time, the endless season of snow and rain storms, the moment of white flowers, and the weeks when the world was both green and hidden in fog. In large part through her teaching, centered on basketry but extending far beyond, I came to embrace the beauty of these seasons and saw unions of season and place, of place and people, of people and craft.

It was coincidental that my interest in Aleut basketry began as a general rejuvenation of Aleut culture was occurring among Aleut people. Both developed over years, across seasons which supplied the materials and time required. As I came to appreciate this craft, to see it as more than the production of a beautiful object, I was the recipient of great kindnesses from local folks. Their generosity of spirit surfaced in brief meetings with elders; it was revealed in those most intimate of emotions: laughter and grief; it endured as friendship.

Hilda Berikoff had made the 150-mile trip from Unalaska to Cold Bay to witness the marriage of her son Alex to Marie Tcheripanoff. There was no priest resident at Unalaska, but a marriage by Magistrate Maggie MacNiece would suffice until a priest visited. The event appeared as a note in Anfesia Shapsnikoff's diary, which years later, her sons and grandson gave me after her death. On August 22, 1964, she had written, "Alex and Marie got married and back [August] 21." I date my arrival by this brief note about a marriage tragically shortened. On December 23 of the next year Anfesia wrote, "Alex Berikoff disappeared found only boat next day." He had taken his skiff to hunt ducks in Captain's Bay. People speculated the recoil from his rifle had caught him off-balance, thrown him overboard. In that cold water, especially during winter months, life ends in minutes.

For all its dangers, the sea remains a second home for Aleuts. The trail to Ugadaga was more correctly the trail from Ugadaga. It was used when someone needed to get to Unalaska Village and the water was too rough to go by boat around the headlands. Its use in pre-European contact times is conjectural. Why would anyone need to hike overland when the circumference of the island was dotted with villages?

Aleuts had lived in the islands for over eight thousand years when Russians arrived in the Eastern Aleutians in 1759, eighteen years after Vitus Bering's voyage of discovery. By 1775 a trading settlement had been established at Unalaska by Ivan Solov'ev, and here men from Captain James Cook's vessels visited in 1778. By 1791 Grigorii Shelikhov's rapacious company had established its own post in Unalaska's protected harbor. A trail from Ugadaga Bay to the Unalaska settlement was in use by 1805. In July of that year Nikolai Rezanov, friend of czars and representative of the Russian-American Company, found himself trapped by foul weather in Beaver Inlet. Anxious to visit the settlement, he readily agreed to follow Aleut guides overland and set off accompanied by two of his lieutenants, his physician, and others. Of course the trail did not end near the summit of the pass as it does now but continued down the mountain, across the valley, along the lake, and eventually onto the peninsula where the small settlement had been located. The story that Russians ordered Aleuts to lay boards in front of Rezanov so his feet stayed dry is not confirmed in the account written by Rezanov's physician, G. H. von Langsdorff:

> Several lovely little flowers were blooming along the shore . . . the low-lying areas of a nearby valley were covered by high grass. I had no time to dwell on the newness of everything as I would have wished: the jagged, rocky crags with conical, snow-covered mountains behind them, the slopes we had to climb up only to climb down again into the next valley. Soon night fell. Guided by several Aleuts, we made our way in

*the dark through that pathless terrain. Cliffs and boulders, fox holes,*
*bushes, and piles of rocks made walking difficult. Near the end of our*
*difficult hike, one of our companions, happily thinking he had*
*discovered a footpath, ended up standing in a creek over his knees.*
*Finally, toward midnight we arrived in Illuluk tired and exhausted.*

In the eighteenth and nineteenth centuries, Unalaska village was called variously Illuluk, Iloolook, and Iliuliuk. As the major settlement on the island, this village gradually adopted the island's name for its own. The island's unorthodox name had evolved from the Aleut *Nawan-Alaxsxa* or *Nagun-Alaxsxa*, whose meaning is uncertain but may contain the original name for Alaska preceded by a demonstrative. The name had changed from *Agunalashka* to *Oonalaska* and finally, with many variants in between, to Unalaska. Older Aleuts I knew continued to say Uu-nalaska, eschewing the negative prefix of *un*answered, *un*profitable, and *un*tamed.

In the 1830s, the Ugadaga trail was called *General'skii* in honor of Rezanov. Saint Innocent of the Aleutians, Ioann Veniaminov, recorded this local name and used the trail himself at least four times. The first was on June 12, 1827, when the vessel he was aboard anchored in Beaver Inlet at 6 A.M. after spending the entire stormy night under sail within the inlet. Veniaminov left the ship in a *baidarka*, probably in an *uluxtax̂*, the Aleut two- or three-man skin boat in contrast to the one-man vessel called an *iqyax̂*. He landed at Ugadaga Bay.

"From there I hiked over the mountains with a guide," he wrote. "After covering about ten versts, I arrived home in [Unalaska] at one o'clock in the afternoon."

The initial two decades of hostilities between Aleuts and Russians in the Eastern Aleutians, roughly 1759 to 1779, gave way to another two decades of coexistence. In 1799 the Russian American Company was granted its monopoly over all Alaskan commerce and Aleuts discovered themselves dominated by a ruthless bureaucracy. In 1824 Father Veniaminov began his ten-year mission at Unalaska. Although economic conditions for local people did not improve, this period witnessed the transformation of much of the Aleut population. Under Veniaminov's tutelage, children attended school, literacy in Aleut and Russian flourished, Aleuts became the administrative and spiritual backbone of the Orthodox church in Alaska. Educated Aleuts began to fill important positions as teachers, navigators, draftsmen, administrators, and priests. By the time the United States purchased Alaska in 1867, Aleuts were, indeed, as documents of the day worded it, a "civilized tribe" deserving citizenship and the vote.

But Americans anxious to strike riches in the new territory objected to any indigenous population with claims to land or commerce. In 1869 Aleuts who were visiting San Francisco, where the Orthodox church was establishing a headquarters, made a presentation before the chamber of commerce and said, ". . . we have been granted by his Imperial Majesty, the Czar of Russia, all the rights and privileges enjoyed by the merchants of Russia, and which we here enjoyed until the change in the government; but now, being annexed to the United States of America, we are deprived of these rights and privileges. Our brethren, the citizens of the Great Republic, look upon us as wild Indians, but we are not savages. We had formerly our schools, and our rights and privileges, but now have nothing."

In the 1880s, Protestant missionaries arrived in the wake of whalers and pelagic sealers. Which was worse: the evangelical fervor of missionaries intoxicated with righteousness, or the venal fervor of sailors just plain drunk and out for a good time? While the latter's damage was quick and sometimes violent, the former's influence gradually eroded the foundations of community and family solidarity as they worked to eradicate all vestiges of Native life and the Orthodox religion. It is no wonder Aleuts affected a studied indifference to outsiders.

From the late nineteenth century well into the twentieth, the Ugadaga trail was used by people from Biorka village, located across Beaver Inlet on Sedanka Island. With the introduction of wooden skiffs and dories and the gradual abandonment of the *iqyax̂* and the *ulux̂tax̂*, the trip around the northeast end of Unalaska Island was replaced by a run across Beaver Inlet. The skiffs were left at Ugadaga Bay, and people walked overland to sell furs and purchase supplies.

Anfesia Shapsnikoff told me that in the 1920s and 1930s, the Biorka people would come to town and before doing anything else they would pay their respects to the chief and to the church warden. The hike back, although more gradual, was more arduous because sacks of flour and sugar and clothes from the mission house were heavier than bundles of fox fur. The Biorka people made this trek regularly before World War II. Afterward, after the evacuation of Aleuts from the islands and their eventual return, the trail was used less. The Biorka people were moved to Akutan and Unalaska.

Andrew Makarin led an effort to reestablish the village; but whether because of military pollution or the natural cycle of the resource, fish had virtually disappeared. The price for fox fur had plummeted. The pull of conveniences at Unalaska had won, and Biorka was abandoned. The trail was then rarely used, and Andrew pulled his skiff high into the grass, out of the reach of storms.

I finally left the pond near the summit and started down the trail to Ugadaga Bay. The September outing provided a descent through seasons: Thin echoes of spring gradually were covered by the efful-gence of the end of summer. Where the trail began, there were still late blossoming iris, their purple rags gathered into gold knots. Spent blooms drooped like wax. While most had berried, a few mock dog-woods blossomed, their four white petals stained reddish brown. Blue violets and purple orchids were rare now, but spindly narcissus anemones still flowered late, desperate, wildly articulated. The trail wore through fractured rock where silver and black lichens attacked the undisturbed surfaces. With a growth speed about zero, these single-petaled, black, petrified roses took decades to reach a two- or three-inch diameter. Locked inside them was a deep magenta dye. Among the rocks delicate heathers grew with their lanterned blossoms and varnished leaves so diminutive they formed a short-napped carpet.

By autumn the thin grasses growing among the shoals of heather had turned gold. When the light was right—and the wind was always blowing—they flickered across the green heather like the hairs on my arms.

The trail dipped steeply below a triangular peak and edged an embankment opposite a broken waterfall. Pea-green moss grew in rich clumps among the water-blackened rocks as the water fell into a deep bowl. The trail dropped to where the creek was easily forded. Here with luck I might have found the last ripe unrotten salmonberries in protected gullies. And in the final feat of summer, sparse monkshood bloomed. With the approach of autumn a swatch of cotton flowers gradually unraveled across a protected swamp. Wide-leafed wild celery, the whiteness of their ferocious blossoms gone to seed, guarded the borders with stalks of aristocratic sureness.

The head of Ugadaga Bay was skirted by a U-shaped valley. On my first hike I took a rough sighting on the center of the beach and dropped as rapidly as possible to the flats only to be buried in grass and brambles. The small creek I had earlier jumped across had been fed by springs and attending streams, and now determined never to reach the sea, it twisted unendingly. Too deep to wade, too wide to leap across, it suddenly funneled under a mound of sod, reappeared, and circled back.

I struggled over humps of receded beaches, fought dense grass, tripped over roots, and landed with my palms cut by the needled points of the inner blades of wild rye. The grass was at its luxuriant finale. The inch-wide blades, extending over five feet long, were starting to brown along their tips and edges. Periodically a blond head of rye towered out of the full avalanche of grass. This, although I did not know it at the time, was that perennial staple of Aleut culture: basket-weaving grass.

As I pushed myself back up I saw the rusted tip of one of the curled iron posts inches from my head. Decades of rampant growth and decay had absorbed all but its harpoon-like point. After that tumble I altered my steps. My first trek across the flats was my last.

If it weren't for the convenient trail, Ugadaga would rarely be visited as it is a remarkably dull bay. Gently sloping, pebbled with monotonous stones, depressingly free of debris, the long curved bay eventually reached the south side where the stream finally broke from the valley and flattened, I think in resignation, as it coursed across the beach. Approaching the south side of the bay's mouth, I was grateful for cliffs and outlying rocks, but before long I found myself with an unpleasant choice. The tide had coated the upper beach with a thick layer of rotting kelp. One awkward step made clear how slippery it was. Below the kelp line every rock was crusted with thousands of petite snails. Unwilling to backtrack I walked forward crunch by crunch.

Past the kelp and snails, boulders began crowding the beach. At the southeast entrance of the bay, a descending mountain dipped into a narrow tongue scalloped on both sides by curved pebbled beaches. The short peninsula abutted an outcropping of rock, a green mound, walled by vertical cliffs like a medieval bastion. Tenacious grass and ferns were wedged into crevices above the high water line. In the thicket leading to the beach, I'd seen the spent remains of watermelon berries, wide leaves and stems drained of all energy. On the beach were other finds. Two plastic buoys. A tangle of plastic rope braided with seaweed. Broken teeth of incorrigible Styrofoam. A square, clear whiskey bottle. An empty amber Japanese cough syrup bottle with a tiny whale embossed on its base. I rinsed this jar and slipped it into my pocket.

A dampness blew out of the southeast across Beaver Inlet and back toward the Ugadaga trail. The first autumn storm would soon rake the hills, dropping temperatures, stripping leaves from blueberry bushes leaving branches clustered with indigo fruit: a favorite berry-picking time. It was impossible to hurry returning over the boulder-crusted beach, and by the time I had waded the shallow stream and begun the trek along the head of Ugadaga Bay, the rain had started. I reached the trail on a low ridge on the north side of the bay through a tangle of grass, willows, and ferns.

Once on the path I made good time, the wind at my back billowing my poncho. I crossed an immense carpet of mossberries, *Empetrum nigrum*. Dark berries were scattered like marbles. With one scoop I brought a handful to my mouth and crushed out the slightly acidic juice before spitting the seedy residue to the ground. Cooked they made a delicious rich sauce, but I quickly abandoned the thought of carrying any back to town.

The downpour drenched the smoke-like seeds of fireweed but couldn't obscure the few remaining fuchsia blossoms. The leaves near the base of this abundant plant were dark and curled as though burnt, but rising along the stalk they broadened, singed in glorious orange and red and lingering green. I gave one more glance backward and downward toward Ugadaga Bay. The sheets of rain moving up the valley opened, and for an instant the outline of Andrew's skiff appeared in the grass, and then it sank from sight.

## 2
# Village Lives, Village Elders

Gaunt and aristocratic George Borenin was chief of Kashega village, but Kashega had ceased to exist. With its harbor, lake, and stream, this bay on the southwest coast of Unalaska Island had been the site of an Aleut village for centuries, but by the beginning of the twentieth century, loss of sea otters and fur seals had eroded the economic basis for community life. Attempts at sheep-ranching proved insufficient to prevent people from drifting to Unalaska.

Following their World War II evacuation the Kashega people settled elsewhere—primarily at Akutan and Unalaska. However, George Borenin and Cornelius Kudrin (assisted for a while by Mike Kudrin of Akutan) returned to their village after a stay at Unalaska.

Although George had been chief of the community, more importantly he was the reader in the church, and his return was to safeguard the small chapel dedicated to the Transfiguration of Christ.

I have seen two photographs of George taken at Kashega in the mid-1950s by the anthropologist Theodore Bank II. In one, George is seated in front of a large short-wave radio. In the other, he stands inside the church, his shoulders slightly stooped, the altar railings glow with fresh paint, Christ stares at the camera from an icon.

Like other Western institutions, the Orthodox church determined to change Aleut lives and did so. Unlike commercial companies and governmental bureaucracies, Russian and American, this change was primarily effected by soliciting and receiving the assistance of Aleut people themselves. Undoubtedly Aleut conversion to Christianity was speeded both by the Russians' effective suppression of recalcitrant leaders and by the Russian fur hunters' lay baptism of wide portions of the Native male community. (With these baptisms came the adoption of Russian names.)

Nevertheless, it is to Aleut leaders from the late eighteenth to the early nineteenth centuries that credit goes for the transformation of their society. Men like Paramount Chief Ivan Glotov of Umnak, Paramount Chief Nikolai Dediukhin of the Andreanov Islands, and the chief and linguist Ivan Pan'kov of the Fox Islands spearheaded this conversion. Their work led to such prominent nineteenth-century Aleut priests as Iakov Netsvetov, recently canonized, Innokentii Shaishnikoff of Unalaska, and Lavrentii Salamatov of Atka. Consequently, when the 1917 Russian Revolution first curtailed and subsequently halted the assistance of the Mother Church, locally educated Aleut leaders naturally assumed positions within their religious communities as readers, deacons, choir leaders, and priests.

As staunch Christians, Aleuts saw little reason to leave the church of their ancestors to join the very white and very well-connected congregations of Protestants who, arriving as government teachers and commissioners, found everything Aleut both unpleasant and foreign. The response of local people to this almost hostile proselytism was "We just don't bother with them." Sooner or later they would leave. But when the teachers and missionaries showed an appreciation for the culture and an empathy for the harsh conditions early in this century—missionaries like Dr. Albert Warren Newhall and his wife Agnes Sowle Newhall, who devoted their lives to the community—they were welcomed with friendship.

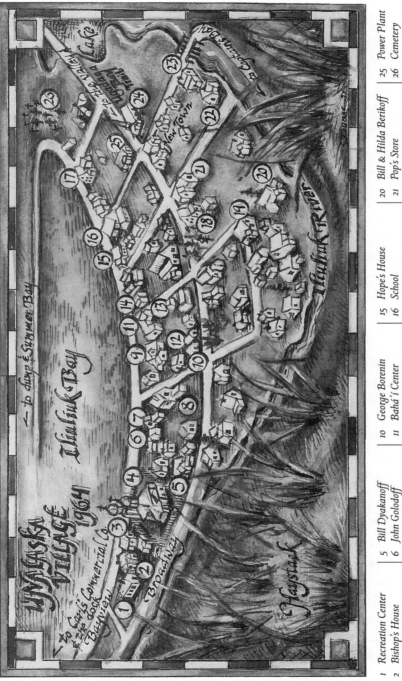

# UNALASKA VILLAGE 1964

Ilieliuk Bay

Haystack

Iliuliuk River

← to dump & Summer Bay

to Carl's Commercial Co. & the dock — Bayview

1 Recreation Center
2 Bishop's House
3 Alaska Salmon
4 Church of the Holy Ascension

5 Bill Dyakanoff
6 John Golodoff
7 Agnes Chagin
8 Elbow Room
9 Nick & Polly Lekanoff

10 George Borenin
11 Bahá'í Center
12 Henry Swanson
13 Aleutian Mercantile
14 Marshal's House

15 Hope's House
16 School
17 Jesse Lee Home
18 Alice Moller
19 Anfésia Shapsnikoff

20 Bill & Hilda Berikoff
21 Pop's Store
22 Andrew Makarin
23 Sophie Pletnikoff
24 WWII Chapel

25 Power Plant
26 Cemetery

After Mike Kudrin moved to Akutan (there was already a different Mike Kudrin living at Unalaska), George and Cornelius found their increasing ages made living difficult at Kashega, and they decided to move back to Unalaska and end a feud that had sent each man to row his own skiff out to the mail boat to collect his own mail. George's niece and grandniece now had homes at Unalaska, and Cornelius's relatives also lived there.

The icons from the Kashega church were removed by Father Nagosky and placed in the Church of the Holy Ascension at Unalaska for safekeeping. Cornelius found a small house near the creek. George moved into a cabin that Jeb and Elaine Caldwell made available to him for life.

The Caldwells and their three young boys had moved to Unalaska in 1953 to establish an outpost for the Bahá'í Faith. Eyebrows were raised after Jeb answered the question "Are you a Christian?" with "Of course. And also a Moslem and a Buddhist." People suspected that another religion was not what the community needed. In ten years the Caldwells built a Bahá'í Center out of three World War II cabanas and established the town's first king crab cannery. They settled in the Aleutians as the result of a worldwide expansion plan conducted by the Bahá'í Faith, and among the first things they did was to ask a surprised telegraph operator to send a wire to Haifa, Israel, reporting their arrival. Shoghi Effendi, Guardian of the Bahá'í Faith, cabled back four words: "Loving prayers surrounding you."

In 1953 the Bahá'í Faith was a little over a hundred years old. It had originated in Persia and centered around the life and teachings of Bahá'u'lláh (1817-1892) whom Bahá'ís considered the most recent in a series of manifestations of God that included Krishna, Abraham, Moses, Buddha, Christ, and Mohammed.

I had become a Bahá'í during my sophomore year in college, and after moving to Seattle to attend the university, I had met Jeb Caldwell. It was Jeb who told me about Unalaska and suggested I apply for a teaching position.

The Caldwells had moved away by the autumn of 1964, and the caretakers at the center were two elderly women and an itinerant crab fisherman. The apartment the school board had reserved for me had been rented to someone else, and I was asked to sleep on a cot in the attic of a house rented by two other teachers. So much for being on my own.

After two weeks I carried my few belongings to the Bahá'í Center, increasing its occupancy to four. Vern Zuehlsdorff spent most of his time on a crab boat and his room had bunk beds. Moving in with Ruth Perez and Addie Nordstrom was like inheriting two diverse grandmothers. Ruth played a terrific honky-tonk on the center's old piano and loved to tell stories—especially one that placed her in a Chicago bank when John Dillinger and his gang arrived to make a withdrawal. She had come to Unalaska to join her daughter and son-in-law, Ruth and Gordon Craig, and their teenage children. The Craigs lived at Captain's Bay, two miles west of town, at the crab cannery where Ruth Perez also worked.

Ruth and Gordon had taken Addie Nordstrom into their home in Washington state after the deaths of her husband and only child, and following the time she served cookies flavored with kerosene. It had become clear to her friends that she could not live alone. They had been offered a job at Unalaska but turned it down until Addie insisted they take it and that she go with them. She said her enlarged heart aggravated the pronounced hump on her back, which made her balance precarious. She had learned to relax in mid-fall, however, and her inadvertent tumbles never resulted in broken bones. Almost always confined inside and occasionally to her bed, Addie nevertheless became a favorite of villagers who respected her age, her open, sympathetic reticence, her humor.

In late September, a few days before my roommate Vern moved permanently back to Seattle, he and I were walking down Broadway on a rainy afternoon. In 1964, the village of three hundred people had two primary streets that ran the length of the peninsula: Broadway and Bayview, both unpaved. Bayview began along the beach in front of Carl's Commercial Company's general store (the old Alaska Commercial and Northern Commercial Company stores). With a buffer of rampant grass and lupine between it and the sea, the road followed the curved bay past the empty Bishop's House, the derelict Alaska Salmon Company store, the Orthodox Church, the Shaishnikoff houses, the Golodoff and Chagin homes, Nick and Polly Lekanoff's home, the Bahá'í Center, the three-storied abandoned marshal's house, the pink apartments, and Hope's place. The last two had cement World War II bunkers near them. The road continued past the school, a few more houses, the empty Jesse Lee Home orphanage, on around the corner by the village cemetery and out past the dump. The dump wasn't used much. Few people had cars or trucks or any other way of hauling trash. We threw our garbage into the bay when the tide was going out and turned the dump over to rampaging salmonberry bushes.

Broadway began at the dock, followed the river in back of some old warehouses, the rear of Carl's, the front of the Bishop's House, until the peninsula widened slightly at the Orthodox Church and the road bisected the town. It passed several houses including Bill Dyakanoff's, Joe Lekanoff's, Tiny and Nellie Bereskin's, the old priest's house, the haunted house, John and Eva Tcheripanoff's, George Borenin's, a World War II Quonset hut, Henry Swanson's, the abandoned house where a family had died from drinking toxic alcohol, Alice and Paul Tutiakoff's, the Aleutian Mercantile store, Matfey Petikoff's tiny house dwarfed by an empty immense roller skating rink, a grove of trees, Mrs. Moller's house, the snake pit—so named because of the DTs its various residents experienced—Pop Hortman's store, the backyard of the school, New Town (World War II cabanas hauled down to provide homes for people resettled at Unalaska from other villages after the war), an empty military chapel surrounded by conspicuous trees, and then along the lake and into the valley past innumerable decaying military buildings. Eventually it wound up the hills, beyond the start of the Ugadaga trail, and down into the back of Summer Bay Valley.

Vern and I were a pair of stilts, but Vern was even taller than I and had such a full beard and such piercing eyes that he was sometimes mistaken for a visiting Russian priest, an effect he did nothing to diminish by wearing a long, dark woolen coat. The belted GI surplus raincoat I wore wrapped itself around me in the blowing rain. As we passed George Borenin's, Vern whispered, "Quick! Say hello."

A diminutive woman, obscured beneath a black hooded raincoat, had suddenly darted past.

"That," whispered Vern as the raven-like figure disappeared down a side street, "is Anfesia Shapsnikoff. For all practical purposes she runs this town."

George Borenin lived kitty-corner to the Baháʼí Center and sometimes Addie and Ruth sent me over with a plate of hot food. His cabin had two rooms. The living room/kitchen had a wooden table, two chairs, a sink and a stove. Beyond an open doorway was a small bedroom with a single bed. The cabin could be murderously cold in a prolonged north wind.

George gave me a calendar reproduction of a painting of the Unalaska Orthodox church in winter. The majestic white triple-altared cathedral with its three-storied bell tower and double cupolas rose between the creek and the bay, dwarfed by the layered, snow-covered mounds of Mount Newhall. The artist, Perry Acker, had mistakenly painted the crosses crowning the copulas without their distinctive Orthodox slanting bars. No smoke rose from the stacks of the snow-covered houses, and except for two people hesitating before the open churchyard gate and another figure entering a house, the village seemed deserted.

George would die in 1966 and be buried at Unalaska. The house he had lived in was sold and rented. Twenty years later, after the Kashega chapel had crumbled into a pile of rubble, crushing the lattice of its iconostasis, burying the turned posts of its altar railings, its small cupola was brought to Unalaska and placed in the churchyard.

George's neighbor, Henry Swanson, always older than everybody, referred to George's house as "that shack" and said it was where the cannibal had lived, "oh, sometime in the thirties, before the war." She had been a woman from up north who murdered and ate her husband and moved to Unalaska where she lived "with a fox trapper and a whole houseful of people" before eventually being arrested.

The "church in winter" calendar returned to George's house when I moved in with Shelly Drake, years and many baskets after the events in this account. Shelly had taught first grade at Unalaska for six years and was renting George's old house when we were married in 1978. We objected to Henry calling our home a shack—it was every bit the house that Henry's was. The cabin now sported a bathroom and a front hall which contained an upright freezer, a refrigerator without a door, and a shower. When coats and rain gear were hung on nails opposite these conveniences there was just room to squeeze through—always ducking to avoid the bare light bulb in the low ceiling. We kept rats somewhat at bay by plugging their holes with Tabasco sauce bottles. We couldn't do anything about the cannibal. However, the house was unable to hold Shelly's stuff and my stuff and our wedding presents, and eventually we moved out.

Sixty-nine years old in 1964, Henry Swanson had long been the town's storyteller, a position he would continue to hold for more than twenty-five years. His mother was related to the family of the Aleut priest Innokentii Shaishnikoff. Her father had immigrated to Alaska from Germany, and Henry grew up around his grandfather's stories of sea otter trading in the late nineteenth century. After his Swedish father drowned, his mother married a noted Arctic whaler, and through his influence the young boy was able to participate in the last legal sea otter hunt in 1910. In 1915 he enlisted in the U. S. Navy and served in Hawaii and Panama before his duty on a cruiser and destroyer in the North Atlantic. In the 1920s and 1930s, he was active in the blue fox trapping which dominated Aleutian commerce. With his own vessels, he became more familiar with the islands and waters in the Aleutians than perhaps any other person.

At the outbreak of World War II, the military recognized Henry's intimate knowledge of the area, and he ran vessels used in mapping the islands and in establishing and supplying outposts among the Eastern, Central, and Western Aleutians. After the war Henry remained at Unalaska, where he served for many years on the city council. He took odd jobs as the community reestablished itself after the overwhelming military presence withdrew and the Aleuts returned from their exile in Southeast Alaska.

Although born and raised in the Aleutians and of Aleut descent, although wise, generous, and skilled, at first acquaintance, Henry did not appear to be a bearer of any traditional "Native" wisdom or crafts.

With his navy blue skull cap, his rough weather-resistant jacket, his slate-blue eyes and complexion always slightly sanded by the wind, he seemed very much a fisherman and trapper in the tradition of those Scandinavian immigrants who settled in the Chain in the late nineteenth and early twentieth centuries.

Although he never denied his background and always defended the rights of Aleuts to control their lands and waters, he was often taken for just another white fisherman who had grown old in the islands. He was a puzzle I never solved. I doubt that he was, as I once heard him confide to an unsuspecting visitor, the last person to swim the hundred and thirty miles of icy water from Cold Bay on the Alaska Peninsula to Unalaska. He said he took time out for lunch at Akutan. I have no doubt, however, that he did allow a bored bureaucrat to persuade him to go on a bear hunt while the man waited three days for the next plane off the island. That particular visitor, however, bragged about his impending hunt the night before in the local bar and stormed at Henry the next morning, "Why the hell didn't you tell me there weren't any bears on this island?"

"Well," Henry said, "You were making so much noise about bear hunting that I agreed to take you. You never asked if there were any bears."

Henry was not like George Borenin and the other elderly men who lived alone, displaced from abandoned villages: Kashega, Makushin, Biorka. I saw them collecting driftwood on the beach, returning from washing their honey-buckets in the outgoing tide, fishing in the creek, leaving someone's house. They taught me that however much I learned about these islands, I would never comprehend what the loss of a village meant to village people.

Perhaps Polly understood. She was from Kashega but was younger than these men by a generation. As a child in the 1930s she had contracted a serious eye infection and to secure medication her father, Mike Kudrin, had repeatedly made the long trip to Unalaska traveling from Kashega to Portage Bay by dory and then hiking overland to Captain's Bay and into town. Polly was married to Nick Lekanoff whose own family had moved from Makushin village to Unalaska just before World War II. She and Nick were now raising their own nine children.

At Unalaska Polly would take her uncle's buckets of sea eggs and chaitins. The yellow egg masses from sea urchins and the sweet leathery tongues of chaitins were favorite Aleut foods. The old men received from relatives and neighbors a host of local foods: fish pie made with rice, salmon, eggs, and onions inside a flaky pastry shell; fried bread, *alaadiks*; sea lion and darker seal meat; spring bird eggs gathered on rocky islets; *taaĝux̂*, a tasty dessert made from a mixture of boiled fish or cooked milt, berries, and seal oil.

Polly was an antidote to outsiders' complaints about Unalaska's remoteness, its abundance of weather, its lack of amenities. She was one with whom the island continually shared secrets that she quickly passed along.

"Isn't this the most beautiful place!" she would exclaim whether the evening sun electrified the western banks of Mount Newhall or fog and clouds clogged the bay. She and Nick lived next door to the Bahá'í Center, and many evenings she came over to find out how her three girls had behaved that day in my first- and second-grade classroom. We'd sit and watch the changing colors on the bay, sip tea, and talk. If Ruth had to work the next day, she would soon excuse herself. Before long I, too, would go off to bed, and Polly and Addie would chat into the night. Sometimes she brought over pieces of fish pie or fried *alaadiks*. Once she came with a baked sea lion heart, so delicious, mild, and tender. When buttercups ran rampant in her yard, while I obliterated them with a lawn mower from the Center's yard, she'd laugh as she shook her long dark hair and say, "You're going to make it rain!" And, of course, it always rained.

Like all of us she sometimes cried and fought and had her doubts. She was the first to teach me about the centrality of place in defining who we are. What could I teach her children? That place, by itself, was not enough?

The schoolhouse had been built around 1932 along the beach road. Wooden steps led to a small enclave supported by two wooden square pillars. The door was bordered on each side by a vertical row of square windows and led into an L-shaped hallway off which were four classrooms. At the hall's end on opposite sides of an emergency exit were two bathrooms and steps leading down to the basement, where a huge furnace brooded. Each classroom was banked with paned windows and as the building sat perpendicular to the beach, each room had an angled view of the sea. The first- and second-grade room was to the left of the entrance and looked across the play field toward the church.

The first thing I did when I got to the school was to see if the teaching supplies my Aunt Annie Wake had given me had arrived. For as long as I could remember, she had been a primary teacher near Seattle and she had generously provided me with dozens of suggested lessons, lists of essential reading vocabularies, and numerous simple but effective holiday art activities.

Only my ignorance prevented me from doing more harm than good. There was still a prevalent educational attitude that romanticized and denigrated Native culture. The places teachers came from, the places teachers talked about, the places teachers praised, were not this place.

This place had storms and ice that crusted ships and tidal waves. This place had chiefs.

Bill Dyakanoff was chief of Unalaska and lived alone in a small house surrounded by a rich grove of salmonberry bushes that spilled across the churchyard fence. Known to everyone as "Doc," he was a gentle and generous man whose features were uncreased by age. The strength he'd reaped from years of fishing, sealing, and fox trapping had retired into measured equanimity. Nothing about him was hurried. Nevertheless when fish were running or berries were ripe, he was often busy at his family's traditional fish camp at Ruff's Bay.

Although less spartan than George Borenin's cabin, Doc's house was simply furnished. A wooden table sat before a window that looked sideways onto the street. He had a black-and-white photograph of Unimak Island's Shishaldin Volcano on the wall. The slopes of the Aleutians' highest peak rose sharply to a plume of smoke slanting in the wind.

Although I would not meet Anfesia Shapsnikoff for another year, any introduction to the chief of Unalaska necessitates an introduction to his church; the two were inseparable. When Anfesia learned I had never been inside the church she asked Doc to take me there. The Church of the Holy Ascension of Christ was originally a small octagonal chapel built around 1808. In 1825, Veniaminov replaced the deteriorated chapel with a stately church that stood until the eroding Aleutian weather forced its rebuilding during the years 1854 to 1858 by Unalaska's first resident Aleut priest, Innokentii Shaishnikoff. Another reconstruction project resulted in the present building's consecration in 1896.

Upon passing under the bell tower with its eight bells through double doors from the narthex (predvor) into the nave, a visitor was overwhelmed by the spectacle of the iconostasis covering the entire east wall and rising from a railed platform (amvon) set a few steps above the wooden floor. Ornamental columns and arches ranged across the triple-doored wall separating the nave from the apse where the altar was located.

Built to accommodate a profusion of icons illustrating verities of the faith, the iconostasis was capped by a mural stretching the entire $37\frac{1}{2}$ feet of the wall. Filled with saints and divided by a series of wooden false columns, this mural was crowned by a painting of the Ascension of Christ surmounted by a small cross. The eye was drawn across the wooden ceiling to a large blue six-sided star. Within each of the six curved arms of the star were three smaller stars, and from the axis of the great star, itself a small white star, extended a stout rope holding a three-tiered candelabra.

The tongue-and-groove beaded walls of the church were hung with icons before each of which a small oil lamp, a lampada, was suspended. A railed curved balcony extended out over the doorway while to the right of the door was an immense raised desk where the warden, Nick Lekanoff, kept his candles and supplies.

The spaciousness of this great rectangular white room, trimmed in sky blue, with its deep red floor, was unbroken by pews. Two benches for the elderly or infirm were against the back wall. On the right a door led to the chapel dedicated to St. Sergei of Radonezh. On the left, through another door, was the St. Innokentii of Irkutsk chapel.

When Doc escorted me into the central nave, I floated rudderless in this sea of icons and decoration. The decisive finality of metal against metal as Doc shut the wooden doors behind us brought me to anchor. Our footsteps echoed across the drum of the wooden floor as a deep incense penetrated my clothing and skin. He showed me where the choir stood on the platform before the iconostasis in an alcove created by a large icon and a mounted banner. He had crossed himself before entering and again before certain icons. After he stopped before one of several tall brass stands to straighten a candle, he motioned me to follow him through one of the side doors of the iconostasis. Here, on the walls surrounding the altar, were more icons.

"Here," I thought I heard him say, "is Judy kissing Jesus."

I looked again.

"Here," he said pointing to another icon, "is God going up to heaven."

I looked at the altar and started to walk out through the open double doors directly in front when Doc's firm grip stopped me.

Anfesia raised her eyebrows when she learned I'd visited behind the iconostasis where only males of the Orthodox faith were permitted. My attempt to barge through the Royal Doors whose use is restricted to priests gave her and Doc another thing to tease about when he came again for tea.

Bill Dyakanoff told me it was difficult being chief when people ignored your suggestions. Whereas thirty or forty years before the Unalaska chief, the versatile and accomplished Alexei Yatchmenef, had exercised actual authority in helping to regulate the community, the structure that accommodated a chief and recognized the value of a council of elders had dissolved. The upheavals of World War II with the Aleut evacuation, the intensive economic domination of resources by outsiders, and the success of an educational system with no room for chiefs, had all contributed to a situation where Bill Dyakanoff, Unalaska's present chief, found his influence less and less effective. The people who had elected him and who understood his position grew older and older, rarely participating in the town's economic or political life. Decisions had been reached through achieving a consensus that reinforced village cohesion. Now economic goals motivated the elected leaders and these goals were often bitterly debated and often resolved without consensus.

George Borenin's village had disappeared, but the dignity of his position remained, and may actually have been magnified through some romantic fallacy. Bill, however, witnessed the erosion of the office of chief while the village seemingly flourished. He saw the growing irrelevancy of a position that he had known to be effective, supportive, and integral to Aleut identity. With leadership dominated by younger men—Native and non-Native—the old men who had been traditional trappers and hunters centered their lives on their families and church.

Traditional women's roles, however, continued. Child care, health care, and assistance to the needy remained central to Aleut society, and in addressing these 'Aleut women came into direct contact with officials in education, health, housing, and public assistance. Power had passed to women.

I soon learned that Anfesia Shapsnikoff was the most vocal and established Aleut leader. Literacy had made her indispensable when people needed to communicate with English-speaking bureaucrats or Russian-speaking church officials. Her roles as president of the Orthodox Sisterhood, as village health aide, as a member of the city council, as a Reader in the church, were enhanced by an aggressive certainty that belied her diminutive body. When crossed, she could be merciless. Friends avoided such confrontations; strangers backed away dumbfounded. I kept my distance.

Aleut women exercised authority by themselves, through their husbands and sons, and most effectively through the Orthodox Sisterhood. This loosely knit organization was most visible when it sponsored public events such as the welcome parties held in the fall for everyone new to the community. However, its most beneficial work was a network of social services from monitoring elderly people to arranging informal adoptions.

Another woman with direct authority was Helen Merculieff, the village midwife. Alice Hope had been midwife and health-care provider for many years before, during, and after the war; now, in old age, she was living in Seattle near her daughters.

One of Henry Swanson's great stories grew out of the time he joined Alice Hope and Helen Merculieff picking salmonberries on the western slopes of Captain's Bay. Not far from Nick Peterson's camp was a thicket of berry bushes that few people made the effort to get to even when the berries were profuse.

"Not too long after the war," Henry said, "let me see, maybe about '46 or '47, there was millions, maybe billions, of bumblebees showed up here. There was also a big berry crop that year. Salmonberry bushes that were old, that hadn't had berries on for years, were loaded that year just from the bumblebees."

In the late fall, "towards the end of the berry season," Henry took his skiff out the creek behind the village and went up to Captain's Bay where he saw two women picking berries.

"There was Old Lady Hope and Helen Merculieff, Leonty's mother," Henry said. "I landed there and they said, 'Jeez, the bumblebees are acting funny here, diving into the ground and this and that.'

"So I started to pick some berries, too, and here they were. They were flying upside down, buzzing around, going in circles, doing stunts. When they tried to fly upside down they would fly into the ground and kill themselves.

"Well," Henry explained, "those berries got old and the sun shined on 'em and the juice turned into wine. The ground was covered with drunken bumblebees! I didn't know they were drunk until finally here was a bumblebee, a sober one, one that wasn't drunk yet. He had just arrived at the saloon. He lit on a berry right in front of me. I thought, 'Gee, I'm going to watch that bumblebee.' Well, that bumblebee sat on that old berry and drank wine for about five minutes and then he took off and, boy, he was drunk! He circled around,

made a lot of racket, flew upside down, and dove into the ground!
The air was just full of drunken bumblebees!"

Helen Merculieff's knowledge was invaluable to a village where
planes came two or three times a week, but not every expectant
mother made the trip to the Anchorage hospital. Added to Helen's
willingness to serve was an infectious buoyancy that prodded even
the most downcast to smile back. I knew her through her grandchildren who were in school. They were children from the families of her
son Leonty, Jr., who had his mother's cheerfulness, and of her daughter Sara, who had inherited none of her mother's carefree disposition.
Sara was the most strikingly beautiful woman I had ever met, and as
I walked into the dark recesses of Pop's grocery store, which she
managed, and my eyes slowly adjusted to the dimness, she appeared
like a living Nefertiti.

Helen was an anchor of goodness and joviality, not only for her
family but for the town. At the beginning of my third year of teaching, when school had been in session about a week, on September 8,
1966, Helen had a coughing spell that escalated into choking. The
abruptness of her death intensified our grief. Anfesia was at her fish
camp at Devilfish Point. Her son Tracy arrived at 3:20 that afternoon
with the news. The day was overcast and drizzly, and Anfesia was
soaked by the time she returned to town.

Helen's funeral was three days later in the Orthodox church. I
stood on the men's side, at the very back. There I could stand or lean
against the railing where the great rope from the chandelier was tied
after descending through a hole in the ceiling. By standing at the rear
I could also be as inconspicuous as possible when the service called
for the faithful to kneel, heads touching the floor. Kneeling was foreign
to my Lutheran background, and I remained standing.

We were given thin white candles which we lighted from each
other's flame. Helen's relatives stood, the women with women, the
men with men, coming together as they began the long procession of
final farewells by us all. Suddenly the brass bells in the tower bawled

scrambled and discordant. To my untrained ear it was a random clanging, a dissonance of grief that drove us from the church.

Forty days after Helen's death, the tidal wave alarm sounded. From on top of the diesel power plant at the east end of town, the siren gave short blasts and long blasts: fire and tidal wave. Few of us could remember which was which, but by early evening the town was being evacuated to higher ground.

The host of abandoned military buildings on the lower flanks of Mount Newhall just above the cemetery were the tidal wave houses. One or two had had meager attempts at repair; most were window-less and stoveless but they were higher than the village and that was what counted.

Unalaska had not experienced a tidal wave itself but there had been close calls. In 1946 an immense tsunami had obliterated the Scotch Cap Lighthouse on Unimak Island. On Good Friday 1964, the great Alaska earthquake and tidal wave had destroyed Valdez and damaged much of Kodiak and Seward. On both occasions Unalaska had only a slight increase in tides.

I can't remember whether Addie and Ruth got rides to the tidal wave houses, or if they stayed up the valley at Alice Choate's home or up on Haystack with Sharon and Billy Robinson—both homes were at higher elevations and took folks in. I ended up in a one-room cabana with all of Polly and Nick's children and a few more. Polly was there but not Nick, and as the sky grew darker, Polly left. I soon realized that there were very few adults on the hill—and most of us were white.

Forty days after a person's death a memorial service was always held, preferably in the person's home. So on October 17, as part of the town was wrapped in blankets, shivering before small smoky fires in the tidal wave houses, the more traditional villagers returned to where Helen had lived, a casual stone's throw from the beach. Anfesia recorded the day in her diary:

> At four P.M. Greg came to tell of tidal wave. Went to Sara's at 6:45 P.M. Started reading [from the Gospels]. Most all left to hills. Held service at midnight and came home. Went to bed with mother.

Greg was her son, Greg Shapsnikoff. Sara's place was the Hope house where Helen had been living with her daughter. Mother was Platonida Gromoff, wife of Father Ishmael, the village priest who was traveling out of town.

I came to see that night as Helen's posthumous joke on all of us, a final illuminating paradox. The secret of understanding place was locked inside this event. First of all, it had to do with practicality and not at all with sentimentality. Anfesia, Andrew, Nick, and others knew—as Henry Swanson sitting at home enjoying another cigarette, a can of sardines and crackers, knew—that tidal waves had never struck the Bering Sea side of the Chain. A tidal wave would occur here when Mount Newhall, Ballyhoo, or Split Top collapsed into the bay. There would be no time for escape. A warning siren meant that we were safe.

It had everything to do with people as participants with a particular place and season, how lives are ordered around natural events: first Dolly Varden along the beach, ripening of blueberries, death of the midwife. Although few if any people could name the traditional divisions of the Aleut year, many people continued to respond to the natural phenomena after which these months or seasons had been named. Of course, this active participation with place drove employers at the cannery crazy when people didn't show up for work because the fish were running or the tides—those rare low tides—were right for clamming.

It meant accommodating change. Children and youth were left in the tidal wave houses, and no one was ridiculed for staying there. No one apologized for leaving.

The return to Helen's home echoed George Borenin's return to Kashega. Although it ultimately did not preserve the village or the church, the arrival of George and Cornelius at Kashega said to history that Aleuts would decide if and when an Aleut village would end. No governmental evacuation for military expediency, no botched executions of half-assed resettlement plans could make that decision. Time's legitimacy conferred that decision on the chief. It came to him through all his ancestors. It came to him through necessity.

We become who we are by being in a place a long time. We become part of place so that never again do we arrive or leave. We stay. We stay always.

3

# The Schoolhouse

As Hilda Berikoff had said on the plane from Cold Bay to Unalaska, I should not expect too much. I had come to teach. School began each fall shortly after high school students left town. After completing the eighth grade, students who wanted more education were obliged to spend nine months away at boarding schools—Mount Edgecombe near Sitka, Alaska, or Chemawa near Salem, Oregon.

Although Aleuts had a long tradition of literacy and education, parents found it painful to allow their young sons and daughters to be gone from town for so much of the year. This absence of teenagers produced an artificial community that speeded the maturity of seventh- and eighth-graders—after all, they were now the oldest kids around.

The village was just beginning to shrug off the economic depression that had covered the Chain since the late 1940s. Local people found low-paying menial jobs at the crab processors, but returning high school graduates found little hope for better-paying futures, and many of them stayed away.

Like a kid dressed in his father's clothes, Unalaska had incorporated under the laws of the territory as a first-class city at the outbreak of World War II. The community had been flooded with construction workers, and a few residents had hoped incorporation would give them leverage for negotiating lucrative contracts with the military. One consequence of the incorporation had been the creation of an independent school district. For years this had been a burden for the town, as it had been unable to raise the money required by the territory and state. Now almost twenty-five years later, the child had grown into an adult, and this dependence of the school on revenues from the city prodded the community to act. The king crab boom was bringing money into town, and members of the city council began discussing ways to take advantage of a potentially large tax base.

Except for the constant presence of the sea and wind, the four teachers in the white building along the beach might have been teaching anywhere. Although the school board had all Aleut members, the school existed apart from the village except on rare occasions when the community used it for public meetings. The teachers were removed from the community, and the community rarely penetrated the cultural and administrative walls erected by teachers and the state's Department of Education.

I walked by myself; explored the surrounding hills with their groves of deserted army buildings; occasionally ventured farther, into Beaver Inlet or up into Pyramid Valley. I had frequent visits with Polly, but rarely met or talked with parents of my other students. The head teacher played cards late into the night, drank heavily, made no overtures of friendship to any of the staff. The other two teachers lived by themselves, planning their departures as soon as the year ended. Their only involvement was to feud with the custodian until he removed the handles from the showers to keep them from bathing. They made friends with a young Aleut man (with a long eloquent Russian surname) until the evening they began a venomous critique of a school board member (a woman with a short Scandinavian surname). To their dismay they discovered the woman was his mother.

The most terrifying task I confronted was teaching beginning reading. Fortunately, my aunt had given me the Dolch list of basic words, and using these I attempted to instill students with sight vocabulary. I also made a stab at teaching phonics. Once playing a game I had students guess a word as I tried to sound it out.

"This word begins with the *duh* sound," I said. No response. "There's a 'gh' at the end." Nothing. I thought I'd try some contextual clues. "It's an animal. Duh. . . gh." Silence. Finally, in desperation, "It goes 'bark, bark.'" To my relief a child waved his hand frantically and when I called on him he proudly announced, "A bumblebee." Let's try something else. Let's fingerpaint. The only paper with a waxed or polished surface was a wide roll of brown butcher paper. The only colors of finger paint were orange and blue. To cut the paper I spread it on the floor and had an inspiration: We'd use our bare feet on the large uncut sheet. I didn't suspect how slippery fingerpaint could be or how long it would take to wash twenty-four small feet in the cold water that dribbled out of the tap in the room. It was February, and Valentine's Day was approaching so we cut the dried painted paper into an apocalyptic heart for the wall.

If I had hoped for any supervision or suggestions from the head teacher, such hope was misplaced. He asked me if I would teach English to his seventh- and eighth-graders while he covered beginning science with my class. With my background in English and philosophy, I jumped at the request to teach a subject I might know something about. When he came into my room, I crossed the hall to his class. I found the teenagers friendly and eager to get on with the lesson, so I released the latch on the map covering a good portion of the chalkboard. It snapped shut with a drum roll uncovering a very unblushing nude centerfold taped to the chalkboard. Let's try something else.

The yard around the schoolhouse was knee-deep with buttercups. Gold blossoms saturated the green field. Years of kids on a swing set, a slide, a small monkey-bar contraption, and a wooden merry-go-round had worn down those immediate areas to beach gravel. A chain-link fence, six feet tall and the length of the playground, separated the school yard from the beach road and occasionally kept balls from landing in the bay. The fence straddled a sunken cement World War II bunker whose narrow windows were a constant invitation.

There were days when we all wore gloves inside to keep our hands warm enough to manipulate pencils or to turn pages. There were days when the surf broke with such force that the building shook with its rhythm. There were days when the snow and wind created whiteouts so severe that parents came with ropes to tie a neighborhood of kids together and lead them home. There were days so glorious we had to escape into the hills to see what we could find.

Each day teachers were required to dispense milk. From a gray-brown box suggesting something left from the war, I poured a gray-white powder into a container of cold water. No matter how much I stirred or shook, the powder merely coagulated into globs surrounded by a dull chalky liquid. Nevertheless, we swallowed our Dixie cups full each day. The second year I learned to mix it the evening before and set it to cool until morning. During the hours of darkness, the wads of dry milk were gradually penetrated by water and the mixture in the morning passed for milk.

A week before December 25, the head teacher remembered that each room was expected to present a skit for the community Christmas program. Although the only song I'd been able to teach my class was "Clementine" we managed to work up approximations of "Jingle Bells" and "Deck the Halls." It didn't matter what the youngest children sang or did; they always won the hearts of everyone.

The program took place in the school gym, a long narrow addition on the south end of the school, entered from the outside or through a short, slanting hall from the head teacher's room. Although the ceiling was low, it served as a basketball court despite a few spots on the wooden floor (known to the home team) where bouncing balls were sucked to the center of the earth. Near the front of the gym, a low stage had been built and next to this stood a fir tree, strung with lights and assorted ornaments. The tree had arrived on the December visit of the *Western Pioneer*, a supply ship out of Seattle.

Everyone in town brought all their gifts to the gym—gifts for families and friends. After the school performances, Santa arrived and passed out presents. He concluded his visit by giving each child a paper bag the school board had filled with fruit and candy. Whenever possible the school board recruited a visitor to play Santa, and if timing was right a few younger children could be convinced that Santa had arrived on the vessel that delivered dry goods, canned goods, and a few of the heartier vegetables.

At the end of the evening, families took large envelopes bulging with Christmas cards from the walls. Each envelope had the name of a family and had been decorated by older students with paint and cut paper. As people had arrived for the evening they had dropped cards into the envelopes of their friends and relatives.

These Christmas programs at the school were a tradition until the community grew too large to accommodate all the presents and cards. One year my class practiced a fancy march to a recorded Christmas medley only to have the phonograph break just before the program. We marched to makeshift drums and Christmas castanets. One year we did a Christmas pageant, an allegorical tale, but all I can recall is contained in a photograph of Okalena Lekanoff. She was in the first grade, a cherub of a child dressed in white, with wings and halo. She stood with others in the middle of the stage. I snapped a photograph; the flash malfunctioned and in the resulting print she stands alone glowing, surrounded by shimmering darkness.

The school was given one day off for Christmas, one day off for New Year's Day, one day off for Russian Christmas on January 7, and one day off a week later for Russian New Year. It was a month of celebrations that included gift-giving, dinners, and parties for the Western holidays, and extensive services and celebrations for the Orthodox days.

Before January 7, the church interior was decorated after a thorough cleaning if not a complete repainting. Certain families, assisted by relatives and friends, prepared their traditional stars for caroling during the days immediately after Christmas. The stars, generally eight-sided, had a wooden frame pegged and tied together (perhaps like traditional skin boats), and covered with white cloth. The star rotated on a shaft at the front of which was a stationary disc containing a picture of the Nativity or some other religious scene. The whole was decorated with paint, crepe paper, artificial flowers, yarn, chains of bright beads. When rotating, the star honored the central scene with a halo of blurred color. Families had to buy or prepare food to have on hand to treat the starring crowds and to give to the charity collections made at the same time. People in the church choir held extra practice sessions.

One evening in early January, Polly Lekanoff came over to escape the never-ending preparations at her home for Russian Christmas and New Year. I said something about being amazed at an Aleut basket I had seen for sale at the Aleutian Merc. Polly winked at Addie and said, "You didn't think dumb Aleuts could make anything so good?"

"Polly!" I scolded. I had heard that self-deprecating phrase too many times. At best I was being paternalistic, but Polly, with her typical generosity, said, "You should ask my aunty if you want to learn to weave."

The next morning I knocked on Sophie Pletnikoff's door in New Town—on the outside door like an idiot. There was no answer, so I hesitantly stepped into her immaculate entryway and rapped on the proper door.

This was opened by a gray-haired woman wearing neatly ironed slacks, a long-sleeved shirt, and buttoned sweater. She looked at me suspiciously through plastic-rimmed glasses until I told her I was her grandson's teacher. She smiled but kept me standing on the porch.

After I made my request she gave her kerchief-covered head a quick shake and fired back, "Ha! No! You have no patience!" She shut the door.

Midway through the year I inherited the city clerk's position from Ruth Craig. The duties were few: Carry two cardboard boxes with the extant city records to the school once a month for the regular meetings, take minutes, occasionally write a letter for the council, and issue tax notices once a year. The council set the tax at $50 for an empty lot and $150 if the lot had a house on it. My salary was $50 a month, more than ample since the position provided opportunities to hear the council members as they digressed into stories.

The best storytellers were Henry Swanson and Verne Robinson. Verne had lived at Unalaska since 1939 when he arrived as a deputy U.S. marshal. After the war he stayed in the community, ran a fishing boat, and opened a general store. Verne sometimes reminisced about World War II, and Henry would listen quietly and then relate Verne's story to something from World War I. Not everything told at city council meetings appeared in the minutes.

Some Friday or Sunday evenings I'd go to the movies. Those were the only nights the theater was open. Saturday evening was generally reserved for church. Theater is perhaps too strong a term for the Quonset hut between Henry Swanson's and George Borenin's where Larry Shaishnikoff showed films. School kids would bounce "Hi, Mr. Hudson" off walls until I'd greeted each of them and exchanged quiet nods with their parents. With one exception children and parents invariably called me Mr. Hudson. The children in the Krukoff family, however, always said, "Hi, Ray-hudson," making my name one single dactylic word. Always. Even when school administrators declared the use of first names undermined authority, the children in this family held their own, always respectful, always spontaneous, and always welcome. "Hi, Ray-hudson!"

The films were projected onto a sheet stretched at the front of the curved building and with only one projector there was a pause between reels. People who had been sitting near the oil heater took this time to move away and cool off while those who had been freezing in the back edged forward. For old-timers in the village, the facilities were very primitive compared with those that existed before the war when the Blue Fox Theater had prospered. But then in those years there were special—softer—seats reserved for the few non-Native residents of the village. Now everyone sat on wooden pews scrounged from a military chapel. The pews were equipped with kneeling benches and these seemed especially appropriate when the films were particularly bad.

Throughout the winter the drawings children made, the pictures they colored, filled me with amazement. For Janice, rejoicing in color, the sky was orange, the sun was blue, and her old man was yellow with a dark brown eye. I watched as Sergie's radiant work gradually drained of color the longer his father was at the Alaska Native Hospital in Anchorage. Finally he refused all crayons and chalk and drew only with pencil. His father came back and colors began to reappear in his work, but his pictures never achieved the intensity they had originally possessed. I marveled at Kenny's memory and how he could bring to life drawings of intimate detail. When he drew a face he always put in the lines about the eyes, the convolutions of the ear. When he drew a seashell it became a maze of chambers. Of course, I had students who like me had to label drawings to distinguish cows from canaries. But why were we drawing cows or canaries?

As spring approached I recognized I had not been a success as a teacher. Some of the children were reading, but given my lack of expertise I suspected they would have learned to read on their own. No parents had complained, but neither had the head teacher nor any board member made any comment whatsoever. When word came that a representative of the State Department of Education had arrived I looked forward to an evaluation. Perhaps he would make suggestions about units or approaches I could try. He greeted me and said, "So, you teach first and second grades?"

"Yes, I do," I answered.

He looked at the expansive view out the windows for a few moments and said, "So, you teach first and second grades."

I waited. He looked at the chalkboard with its half-erased math problems, at the displays stapled to the acoustical tile-covered walls, at the orange-and-blue valentine still dominating the wall near the sink.

He said, "So you teach first and second grades." And then he left. Later, I hoped he had asked Henry Swanson to take him bear hunting.

One of the last things my class did that year was to climb the small hill across the creek from town. Haystack had a World War II road that wound to the top, passing several deserted military build-ings. Green clumps of white flowers, narcissus anemones, spotted the brown slopes where last year's grass laid down a soft rug. We enjoyed the view over the church and into the front bay, the line of mountains on the right extending to Summer Bay, past Split Top, and out to Priest Rock at the northeast corner of Unalaska Bay.

We sat among debris from the war and looked over Amaknak Island to where Eider Point formed the northwestern arm of the great bay. We had started back when suddenly the kids stampeded off the road toward a steeper descent and disappeared over the edge. I heard cries and ran forward in a panic. There they were, careening downhill on their stomachs on the soft and splendid grass. The hill was a perfect natural slide they had long used. They were at the creek checking for Dolly Varden trout long before I arrived.

Getting ready for summer vacation, I wanted to buy souvenirs for my mother and sister. Sophie Pletnikoff spread the nutcracker-like dolls she made from rabbit fur and felt on her table. Later she took to making dolls dressed in traditional Aleut clothing, but the dolls she laid in front of me were of a type made by several Aleut women. Their stiff sealskin bodies were covered with bright felt pants and shirts. Sashes festooned with sequins crossed the shirts while seed beads dotted the felt belts, cuffs, and boots. Faces were embroidered on chamois cloth while fluffs of rabbit fur surrounded the heads. The rapidity of Sophie's work was always evident in the crudely embroidered features by which her dolls escaped the bland sameness found in those of more careful artists.

I selected one and she ordered me to also buy that doll's wife. Then I again asked if she would teach me to weave.

"No!"

"Oh, Sophie. Why not?"

"Aiyaya! You want to make Aleut baskets?"

"Yes. I'd like to very much."

"Aiyaya! Come back next year."

Forget the head teacher and the school board, forget the visitor from the Department of Education. At the end of my first year of teaching, I could not have hoped for a better evaluation.

## 4

# A Summer Hike

Among the bays in Beaver Inlet that carry Americanized versions of Aleut names, Chaluuknax̂ never caught the attention of cartographers. Perhaps this was because it is less a bay than a shallow depression along the coast just north of Ugadaga Bay. Nevertheless, it had all the ingredients for a village site: a fresh water lake, a stream for salmon, a broken beach for mollusks. Gavriil Sarychev noted a village here in 1790, and Veniaminov visited several times in the 1820s and 1830s to perform church functions.

The village had long been abandoned, given over to the rank growths of wild celery and beach grass, when the Zaharoff family had their fox-trapping cabin on the beach near the red salmon stream's outlet. That, too, was in decay when the U.S. military erected a lookout station on the cliffs just south of the cove during the war.

The brief Aleutian summer was reaching its peak as I hiked into a long valley off the north tip of Ugadaga Bay. Fog that had folded itself around the mountains for days had dissolved. Following an inland ravine, I climbed parallel to the shore, avoiding the abrupt cliffs that cut off sections of the beach. Cresting the ridge looking into Chaluuknax̂, I climbed on top of a cement bunker that squatted to its shoulders at the cliff's edge. Quonsets with wooden porches huddled leeward among the relaxed folds of the descending slopes behind the cliff. A wooden water tank stood against a steep bank, a reminder of the GIs' efforts to replicate the comforts they had left behind. Amber and pale blue medicine bottles littered the dispensary Quonset, their labels gone. The rust that consumed Quonsets had also flamed across the hulk of a diesel engine that formerly hauled supplies up rail tracks stretched over the less precipitous slopes. Now its gears and cables gave credence to those artists who forged and provoked found objects into sculpture.

I climbed through a hatch into the hollow interior of the bunker. The stove and metal bunks had rusted for twenty years. The few indeterminate wooden furnishings had rotted. A doorway opened down into the observation room with its three narrow windows giving views along the coast and across the inlet. Midsummer and calm, but inside the bunker the air stayed damp and cool. Carefully I wedged myself out one of the rectangular windows onto the bank just below. As I relaxed into a shallow depression, cushioned by grass, the waters of Beaver Inlet opened around me.

I had returned to Unalaska in early August 1965 after visiting my parents in Yakima, Washington. My father's family had held a reunion in Seattle at the home of his two maiden aunts. They, even more than my grandmother, seemed the daughters of harsh Norwegian immigrants. Formality surrounded the warmth and kindness of their hospitality. They showed us family photographs and it seemed to me they could have stepped unnoticed into the ancient pictures of long dead Norwegians whom the great-aunts had visited in 1907. Except for the two great-aunts and various spouses, those of us at the reunion were all descendants of my grandmother. She had three sisters and three brothers, but only she and a younger sister had married.

At the end of the Depression, my grandmother and five of her children and a friend had slipped out of Williston, North Dakota, at midnight in a '36 Ford so piled with belongings they left behind the chains they would need as they scaled the Rockies. They were in debt; it was twenty below zero. My father and the friend drove for thirty-six hours until they reached Seattle. His father and two other children had arrived on the train four hours earlier, and they all went to Bainbridge Island where Dad's sister and her husband lived. By late summer, however, my father was still unemployed, so he and a younger brother, Roy, rode the rails back to Williston to work in the fall harvest. They arrived on a Saturday; on Friday grasshoppers had eaten the crops. Now thirty years had passed. The uncles and aunts and cousins seemed as colorful and alive, if not as cultivated, as the profusion of flowers that bordered the back lawn of my great-aunts' home.

My mother's parents had immigrated from Norway at the turn of the century. Orphaned by their deaths in 1919 and 1920, the seven children kept the family home in South Dakota and raised one another with a profound sense of independence and mutual support. When aunts and uncles gathered I'd overhear conversations about relatives leaving South Dakota first for the prairies of Canada and later for Washington and California.

My parents met in Seattle, married, and moved to Bainbridge Island. When I was four, they took me and my infant sister Judy and bought a home in Yakima, Washington. Typical of children and grandchildren of immigrants, at best we were settled migrants. I remember as a kid being jealous of the kindness my mother showed toward children of seasonal agricultural workers who lived near us. The unsettledness of her own family gave her empathy. No landscape ever held us long.

Within the collection of my aunts, uncles, and cousins there was no longer a common denominator of place. As older relatives remembered small Dakota towns and fields, these places became for me a ghostly ancestral home made real only by meeting my father's oldest brother and my mother's oldest sister, both of whom had remained respectively in North and South Dakota.

Like a multi-forked tongue Beaver Inlet reaches seventeen miles southwestward into Unalaska Island. Sedanka Island forms half of the south side of the inlet with Udamat and Strait Bays. Amugul, Tanaskan, Final, and Kisselen Bays on Unalaska Island complete the south side. From Erskine Bay, a low pass creases into Makushin Bay on the western side of the island. Completing the northern coast of the inlet are Uniktali, Small, Ugadaga, Chaluuknax̂, Agamgik, and Deep Bays, with English Bay immediately northwest of the inlet proper.

Across the bay from the bunker the mountains of Unalaska and Sedanka Islands blend together where Udagak Strait angled between them. The peaks form one continuous ridge of pitched summits, spikes, spears, stone points, anything sharp; angles of fatality recalling Aleut wars of annihilation. A great unconquered sweep of mountains separated me from the Pacific Ocean.

I sat up and edged forward on my stomach until I could see beyond the ragged shanks of rock to the water, its gray steel surface now emerald and cerulean glass. Acres of bulb kelp were awash near the shore while four sea otters lounged on their backs, buoyant in the languid lift and fall of water. On this still and sunny day, whitecaps took wing: gulls. From a distant bluff, two mature bald eagles banked right, creating their own upwelling currents, and rose in slow arcs. North a staggered series of cliffs led to the open sea where Egg Island and Old Man Rocks rode beyond the inlet's mouth.

Upon returning to the island, I had decided to again ask Sophie Pletnikoff for basketry lessons. I knew a year hadn't passed, but a new school year was about to begin. It was, if I stretched the point, "next year" already when I stepped into an entryway singed with the sweet smell of freshly baked bread. Although summer temperatures rarely climbed out of the fifties, baking bread in an oil range forced open doors and windows. I had contrived an excuse for my visit by bringing a package of raffia dyed in assorted colors.

Sophie invited me in and had me sit at her kitchen table while she took the raffia into an adjacent room. Returning, she uncovered a dish on the table.

"Try it," she said and laughed, "*Alaadiks.* Aleut food."

The oval pieces of fried bread differed only in shape from the tubular "dough gods" my grandmother used to make.

"You know, Sophie," I said as I buttered a wrinkled palm of bread and sprinkled sugar on it, "I'd still like to learn to weave baskets."

She laughed—excessively, I thought—and handed me an open jar of salmonberry jam.

On Aleutian summer shores, an eruption of grass overwhelms the beaches. Growing out of the bleached mounds of past seasons, wild rye, *Elymus mollis*, beach grass, basket-weaving grass, surges wave on wave while a carpet of succulent beach pea creeps from the edge. A stalk of *Elymus mollis* may be three-fourths of an inch thick and contain six or seven blades. The blades grow upwards in a tight curled core and gradually unfold as they increase in length until a mature plant may have a stalk eighteen to twenty-four inches long with leaves extending three to four feet.

Beach grass is coarser than the same grass growing slightly inland in meadows or on side hills where thick growths of ferns force it to full height before the blades thicken. It is with grass from these locations that Aleuts weave baskets of astounding fineness and beauty.

A classical Aleut basket is diminutive, cylindrical, and lidded. Weavers were always on the lookout for small cans or jars with smooth and slightly rounded bottom corners over which their baskets could be stretched when not being woven. These forms, replacing earlier hand-carved wooden molds, ensured the gradually growing baskets kept their shapes. The lids of baskets usually had small knobs.

Basket grass can be harvested from mid-summer until after the first snow, but the time of picking is a major contributor to the quality of grass. The best prepared grass is long, very light in color, pliable and strong. It is collected just as the stalks begin to mature and the heads of grain are unfolding. Grass picked later in the summer, about the time schoolteachers are migrating back to the island, has a coarser texture. Storms in early September may bend and crease the blades, making them unusable and increasing the labor needed to secure a sufficient supply.

By the time snow and freezing temperatures have bleached the stalks, storms have destroyed all but the very innermost blades which protrude upward like knitting needles. Andrew Makarin told Anfesia that the Biorka people gathered these late bleached short spears by snapping them from the ground.

But to pick basket grass in mid-summer was to wallow in a green sea as wind shoved the anchored grass. Crouched low to cut stalks close to the ground, I would hold my breath, submerged as the tapered blades whipped forward like rapids.

Over time Aleuts in the Western, Central, and Eastern Aleutians developed many distinctive traits: housing, hunting, language, clothing, art. Regional variations existed also in basketry and in the preparation of grass. Attu people buried their grass beneath a layer of sand for a few hours so that the absorbed heat would quicken the bleaching of the grass. Atkan weavers spread their grass out on the hillsides to change color. Unalaska women bundled their grass and placed it beneath deep ferns or under the house where it was covered with burlap to keep it dark and damp. At times the stalks were rinsed in salt water to make them stronger as young people were once urged to begin their days by immersion in cold water.

When sufficient green had drained from the grass, the stalks were separated into their individual blades. Generally only the center three blades were reserved for weaving, with the inner blade being considered the prize. The inner blades were as white as halibut, as pliable as string. When dry they could be split with the fingernails into strands as fine as silk. From a bundle of grass so large that the weaver's two arms could barely surround it could be culled a swath of inner strands only as thick as a thumb.

Each group of separated blades—the firsts, seconds, and thirds—were next braided or twined into strands for drying. Sometimes they were placed inside the house in front of windows where the sun could hit them. However, it was not good for grass to dry before it had bleached. Sometimes they were hung outside on lines or placed under fish-drying racks. When placed outside, they had to be monitored so that the rain would not strike them. However, there were times that a heavy rain on the grass helped to wash out darkened spots. The weaver had to calculate and watch.

Anfesia would tell me it was as much work and as difficult to prepare the grass properly as to weave a basket.

I crawled back from the edge and nested again in my bed of grass outside the bunker. The August sun was, of all things, hot. So I took off my windbreaker, put on my sunglasses, and leaned back. In a few minutes I opened my backpack, unwrapped a crisp disc of pilot bread and spread peanut butter on it. As I took a bite I recalled Sophie's fried bread and smiled. Perhaps to keep me from eating all her *alaadiks* and to get me out of her house, she had finally agreed to give me basketry lessons.

The impassibility of the cliffs south of Chaluuknax̂ at all but the lowest tides magnified their height. In reality they reached just into the second community of plants that characterize the topography of the Aleutian Islands. The long belts of beach grass formed the lowest plant association together with beach pea and other seashore plants. In the rocks among pale pea-green clumps of beach pea grew the darker, thick-leafed ragwort with its fists of yellow blossoms. Luxuriantly blossoming spring beauty and fragrant-leafed wild parsley also were found along the shores. Away from the beach, knee-high lupine captured orbs of dew at the center of their palmate leaves. Their blossoms, blue and white and bleeding with purple, tapered like ascending stairs.

Further inland subalpine meadows were thick with flowering plants in midsummer: geraniums of palest blue, blue like veins, pearly everlastings, monkshood rearing their papal stalks, early blossoming low-bush fireweed. The pungent leaves of yarrow grew at the feet of wormwood among ptarmigan grass and paintbrush. *Petruskii*, whose tender leaves and stems added a parsley flavor to soups and fish, grew in thick clumps. More varieties gathered around ponds: marsh marigolds with their round leaves like water lilies; delicate, whimsical monkey-faces, yellow and white, named after Rezanov's physician; and the pride of all fields, purple unblushing iris. Thickets of scrub willow arched out of meadows into ravines. Broad-leafed ferns carpeted the drainage slopes leading to these gullies while black-stemmed maidenhair ferns nestled in protective clumps.

In his *Flora of the Aleutian Islands*, Eric Hulten delineated Aleutian plant associations and wrote, "Above the meadows and the *Salix Barclayi* [willow] thickets, which in the inner valleys of eastern Unalaska reach in some places an altitude of 80-100 m., one finds a mosaic of alpine heaths and meadows, the heaths being most predominant...."

Cascading melodies of Alaskan longspurs floated behind me as the sparrow-like birds coasted onto an alpine meadow. Many of the plants found in lower meadows grew here but with a smaller stature. Here, too, were leather-leafed saxifrage and club-mosses. Protected knolls ignited with Kamchatkan rhododendron, their petals drenched in scarlet stained glass. And everywhere, fallen from heaven, were fields of cornels.

At higher elevations, pure *Empetrum nigrum* heaths cushioned the slopes. Now chiefly a joy for hikers who want somewhere soft to sit, this plant formerly provided Aleuts with fuel and "true" berries. On treeless islands where driftwood was often too valuable to burn, *Empetrum* met an acquired need. The stems, like miniature pine boughs, were fed one at a time into a fire—either to immediately

bring a wide-bottomed kettle to boil or to create an intense contained
blaze inside a small brick oven. The black, slightly acidic berries were
preserved in oil inside a prepared sea lion stomach—or later, they
were stored in wooden barrels filled with water. Near the summits,
the heaths became broken. Wind-sculpted roots and branches
of dwarfed willows lay bleached like bones across flakes of rock.
Thick-veined bluebells of transparent horn clung incongruously to
the slopes.

The Aleutian Islands were so green the whole short summer long
that I was alarmed when any green was gone. Perched at the cliff's
edge, I was flooded with solitude. I became a segment of the world's
curve. The sun opened over me. By god, it was hot, I thought. But
then I thought, these are the Aleutians! But there isn't any wind! In a
minute I had stripped. Cousin to seals, I had become that rarest of
Aleutian land mammals: sunbathing human.

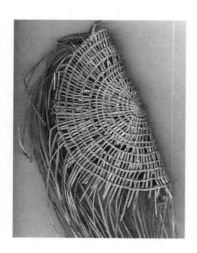

5

# Village Lives, Village Laughter

Sophie Pletnikoff came to Unalaska from Kashega, her uncle George Borenin's village, but she always made clear that she had been born at Chernofski. Sometime in the late 1920s, the people in that village near the southern end of Unalaska Island had packed their personal belongings, crated the goods from their church, and sat on the beach where Henry Swanson found them and brought them to Unalaska on his fifty-five-foot vessel, the *Alasco-4*.

Sophie's reluctance to teach me basketry may have reflected the way she herself had learned, for when I asked who her teacher had been, she said she had just watched other weavers. She had learned by watching.

My first lesson was appropriately brief. We were in her kitchen, where the walls shone with high-gloss paint, the linoleum floor glowed with fresh wax, and every surface that could be polished— including the top of the oil range—glistened fiercely. I sat at her formica table drinking tea and enjoying a slice of fresh bread whose crust had been glazed with milk, while Sophie, sitting across the room, worked furiously at what appeared from that distance to be a snarl of grass. Suddenly she threw it at me and ordered, "Now you do it!"

Sophie's finest baskets carried repeated geometric patterns across their woven surfaces. Bright diamonds, triangles, and squares worked with embroidery thread, balanced or staggered in rows often separated by lines of solid color or lines of open weaving. These designs, red and green, purple and yellow, pink and blue, were anchored in the fiber of the weave, carried the rhythm of the grass, as Henry Swanson's stories were anchored in the islands.

Henry Swanson: *I trapped blue fox one winter on West Unalga. One morning I was making breakfast and talking to my partner. He was still in bed and he didn't answer me. I looked over at him and he was sittin' there glaring at me like he was mad. Well, you know, he didn't speak for three months. He had cabin fever. One day I was away from the cabin. This guy had a sharp ax and he accidentally cut into his knee, real deep cut. Well, I finally got back and my partner was in bed. He was hurt and he needed help, but I decided I wouldn't help him until he spoke. I was going to be mean.*

*Finally he said, "Have you got a plaster?"*

*I didn't have a plaster, but I took a rubber boot and cut off a piece at the top and pulled the cloth lining out of it. I put a gauze pad over the cut. It was a big V of a cut with the bone showing inside. I melted the two ends of the rubber and stretched the rubber band around the knee and connected the two soft pieces. Then I wrapped it.*

*That man laid in bed for twenty-eight days until we got picked up. He talked all day and all night long for twenty-eight days.*

An Aleut basket is woven by twining two weft strands over a series of warp. As the circumference of the base expands, the number of warp rapidly increases. A basket Sophie made with a base diameter of 3 inches began with 4 and ended with 180 warp strands. The 3¼-inch side contained 85 rows, which meant this small container, excluding the base and the cover, had over 15,000 stitches. A larger basket she made had a 4-inch diameter base with 240 warp strands. The 3½-inch sides had 92 rows resulting in over 22,000 stitches on the basket sides. Sophie's work was not considered especially fine.

Henry Swanson: *During the war, I was taking my outpost tender around to Makushin and other points. I left Unalaska and went out through the sub-gate and on around towards Makushin, keeping close to the shore like I always did.*

*Later the army sent for me to come to Adak to be outpost tender. They had a lot of outposts out there and they had Adak surrounded with mines. I got out there, and they gave me a chart of the minefields. I never used their chart. I went in among the rocks and reefs where I knew there were no mines. They had those mines way out from shore clean around Adak; that is, all the places where landings could be made. There was a strip inside of them and that's where I used to run. The mine-layers were big boats, and they couldn't or didn't dare get too close in, so the mines were in deep water. They left a channel through the middle of each minefield—but no marks to find that channel and I was supposed to use those channels. In fog you wouldn't see anything anyhow. But I could always find the reefs at the other end of the minefields, and I'd go around and get inside where I could run around along the beach. I had quite a few outposts that I had to tend inside the minefields.*

Henry could throw away the map because he knew the place before the map was made. And he knew the map; knew what was on it and what was not on it. This is mastery. Many times I've thrown away the map too soon, thinking I knew the country.

Sophie Pletnikoff's baskets have this same sureness. They surface out of stillness with a vigorous jolt. The stitches are uneven. The embroidery thread is too thick or it is wrapped too many times over the weft so that after a few rows the line of weaving begins to wave. Agnes Thompson of Atka, the greatest weaver of our times, wrote that each basket has its own personality and the large one she wove for the Unalaska school fought her every stitch.

Whereas Agnes mastered the basket and produced a work

incredibly detailed and balanced, Sophie's baskets always left a trail of struggle. They have little of the calm, even surface on which the finest weavers create a mirrored design. Her baskets are sea baskets woven against the current of the grass. They carry the energy and beauty of rough water.

Henry Swanson: *That time I was going to Makushin I met two large freighters escorted by a cruiser. The cruiser flashed signals at me and I answered, but my signal light was just a little thing, a regular light, and the cruiser couldn't pick up my signal, so he started to chase me. I was overcome just outside Volcano Bay entering on towards Makushin.*

*I had a new mate, a civilian, who didn't want to work. He just wanted to wear a uniform. I fired him later at Adak. Anyway, I sent the mate out to talk to the two officers on the cruiser. They had a little bridge on each side of the house door and they stood out there and gave my mate hell for quite a while. I finally got angry and stormed out on deck dressed in my dirty, old clothes. I told those officers to get the hell back to their vessels! They belonged out there. I was taking care of the coast! Well, that was correct. Their duty was to escort the freighters, not to chase me.*

*They evidently thought I was someone important dressed in old clothes because both officers tried to get through their little door at the same time. They bounced back onto the deck and both charged for the door again and got stuck and bounced back and finally went into the cabin single-file.*

I painstakingly unwove a few of Sophie's stitches trying to preserve the imprint of the grass in order to weave it back again. This was not what I had expected.

"Now, you do it!"

I didn't know my fingers could sweat so much.

The sun at Unalaska always rises and sets. In the winter six hours or so of daylight, often muffled by clouds, surround the island.

During the summer a brief tent of darkness hides somewhere between extended sunsets and sunrises. Late on summer evenings, mist-laden clouds disperse while the sun still holds above Makushin and the western mountains. Angled light slips inside leaves and stems, light greens and deep greens, greens falling into yellow. The translucent slopes of Ballyhoo and Split Top glow with a lifted warmth and move closer to the village.

In addition to baskets and dolls, Sophie made wall-pockets and small containers from cured seal and sea lion gut. She showed me how to twist fine segments of whale sinew into strands of thread. She built a wooden model of a fish trap and made a replica of an Aleut hanging cradle.

One evening I had my tape recorder going when she tried to explain the Orthodox custom of masquerading. Christmas concluded with days of starring and this was followed by days when people dressed in masks and costumes, and visited their neighbors where the hosts had to try to identify them. It was an occasion for hilarity and celebration. At the close of masquerading, revelers had to wash themselves in the creek in a symbolic act of purification. This needed to be done before entering the church for Epiphany service.

Well, Sophie explained this to me and I didn't understand. She spoke about masqueraders. I replied by talking about muskrats.

"Yes, I've seen them."

"Yes. They go in the water."

But when I said they were small and furry and something like mice, she looked at me strangely.

Henry Swanson: *Seguam Pass was a bad one. We went through there one night going from one side to the other, you know, from Pacific to the Bering Sea. It had got so rough in the Pacific. We had a small boat, too, a fifty-footer. And that same night there was a big ship right out further out at sea from us that sunk while we were going through this pass.*

*We had a big sail on this boat, too, beside a engine. It was fair wind, so we were bucking a head tide. I was standing on the deck, and this George Ermeloff from Nikolski was standing right by the mast, by the rigging. He was the chief there. We shook and a big sea almost turned us over, filled the sail with water, and the boat laid flat on her side. He must of got washed off of the boat because when the boat stood back up he was gone. I thought he got washed overboard.*

*Anyhow, I heard a little noise way up in the air, and he was way up there on top of the mast. He got washed off and the mast of course was lying even with the water and he grabbed the end of the mast and when the boat stood up there he was!*

*We had a tough time getting him down. He just wouldn't let go of that mast.*

It is a common truth that in weaving, warp and weft are equally important. Although almost never seen, the quality of warp determines the strength, the evenness, and the ease of the basket's manufacture.

Jenny Krukoff, an extraordinary weaver from Nikolski village on Umnak Island, said the weavers there had a very hard time securing real beach grass from under the hungry mouths of sheep and they were often forced to use raffia, a serviceable but inferior fiber. When Jenny's supply of grass was small she invariably used grass for the warp and wove with raffia weft strands. Sophie wove with grass, with raffia, with thick thread, and with strands of colored plastic.

Henry Swanson: *I was nineteen when I went into the navy in May of 1915. There was a recruiting station in San Francisco on Market Street, and that's where I went. I went with another guy, and he didn't pass so I went in by myself. My friend was twenty-four years old. He was the one that promoted it, and he didn't pass.*

*Well, I was ten pounds under weight. I thought, "Gee, I'm not going to pass. Well, gee, that's all right." I didn't want to go into the navy anyhow and said to the examining officer, a doctor there, "You say I'm ten pounds under weight?"*

*"Yeah," he said.*

*"Well, I can go then?"*

*"No, no. We're going to keep you. We can fix that up."*

*Well, I was healthy. I guess that's what they wanted. That place was full of big men, and the only ones that passed were the two little runts—me and another guy, runtier than I was. Yeah! Here were these big guys, big six-footers, and they didn't pass.*

*I don't know about now, but sailors were supposed to hate marines. We came back from the Hawaiian Islands where we'd raised a sunken submarine, the F-4. We went on liberty in San Diego. It was a funny place. We had to pass through this vacant land just full of shacks made out of gunny-sack and tin. The first place we come to was a saloon called The Golden Lion. It was a nice, clean place. We stopped in there. 'Course I was just nineteen years old then, I think. No, I was twenty. We wasn't drunkards, but we were sailors and had to go into the saloon like the rest of the sailors. Well, I went in there and there was some marines in there. I went into the noosnick to take a leak and here was this tall, skinny marine. He was about six and a half feet tall. I looked at him and I said, "I'm going to piss on you." And I did. Gee, whiz! He was a big giant. He just stood there. Afterwards when I thought about it I decided I must have been brave to have done that to a marine.*

Sophie lived in a section of Unalaska called New Town, two rows of four cabanas each which the military had transplanted after the war as homes for people relocated from Kashega, Biorka, and Makushin villages. In some cases the people had landed at Unalaska without the option of returning to their home villages. In other cases, they had arrived as teenagers shortly before the evacuation and returned as adults in need of housing. Sophie's two-cabana home was next to the creek and opposite her was Andrew Makarin's house. Also living in New Town were Sophie's sister Dora and her husband Mike Kudrin, Helen and Kusta Lekanoff, Elsie and Arthur Lekanoff, Nick and Irene Galaktionoff and their family, and Molly Lukanin.

I bought my first Aleut basket, a small covered bottle with a triangular design, from Molly in the summer of 1965 when I visited her at the Alaska Native Medical Center in Anchorage. A gentle, sweet, attentive woman, she died much too young. She was from Makushin village.

Also from Makushin, Kusta Lekanoff spent most of his time at the family camp in Captain's Bay while Helen and their children and grandchildren stayed in town. Helen was raised at St. George in the Pribilof Islands. I often walked her home after she visited at the Center. Never in my life have I walked so slowly. But even at this cemented pace she stopped. She stopped and waited. And then we walked. Sophie was right: I had no patience. Helen wrote long, circuitous letters and made intricate colorings of intersecting flowers and rosettes. She was, in the green world of Unalaska, a startling carpet of scarlet rhododendrons.

Sophie's sister Dora Kudrin had Sophie's energy, but in her case it all went into lavishing affection on her grandchildren and in struggling against crippling arthritis. Of her several daughters, only Polly lived at Unalaska, and Polly's children were Dora's delight. Ignoring perpetual pain, she hobbled to the school gym whenever there was a basketball game, especially if a grandchild was playing. With her husband Mike or one of her grandchildren, she walked the length of the village to church each Saturday evening. If she had not shared Sophie's energy she could not have done so much.

I didn't know Arthur and Elsie, although I knew their son Joe. Anfesia noted in her diary on July 14, 1966, "Bill Robinson found Arthur Lekanoff's boat adrift." Eight days later Walter Dyakanoff found Elsie's body, but Arthur's was never recovered. One story said Elsie's wedding ring was on a seat in the skiff. Another suggested that Arthur was now among the Outside Men, the asx̂aadax̂, spectral figures who frequented the perimeter of the town.

Sophie's brother-in-law, Dora's husband, Mike Kudrin, always picked more blueberries than anyone, more than anyone else ever could pick. And his were clean, too; the bucket wasn't full of leaves and sticks. People said he probably had help.

Andrew Makarin protected the perimeter of the town with holy water.

Anfesia's youngest son, Philemon, insisted that if there were Outside Men there had to be Outside Women. When he, Father and Mother Gromoff, and I went on a picnic to the sand spit off Dutch Harbor, Phil walked into the waist-high grass and shouted, "Arthur! You can come in now! Your social security checks are piling up!"

Henry Swanson: *Well, Outside Men, no. Hell, I didn't believe in
Outside Men, but one time there was somebody you could call an
Outside Man. They had three codfish stations on the west end of
Unalaska in the '30s. The stations closed and two guys who were staying
in one station decided to come to Unalaska. They had a dory, a lifeboat
with an engine, and they started for Unalaska but their engine broke
down. They drifted out in the Bering Sea.*

*Months later one of them showed up in Nikolski. He had drifted
ashore on Umnak Island and wandered around the island until he came
to the village on the other end. He was kind of buggy by that time. He
was crazy. He talked about how he and his partner had fought in the
boat, and he said he'd killed his partner. He finally drifted ashore. I
don't know how he survived, but he wound up in the village.*

*Well, he stayed seven days. They watched him because he was kind
of goofy by that time. They gave him a little house to stay in and one
night somebody went in there and discovered he had a big roll of money
and he was burning it. He was throwing it into the stove and burning it.
That night he disappeared, and that's the last they saw of him.*

Outside Men had their origin in bands of Aleuts who refused to
submit to the Russian American Company's stringent regime.
Veniaminov heard about them and in one case imposed a penance on
an Aleut who had fatally shot a "nomadic Aleut" in self-defense.

"Along this chain and along the Alaska Peninsula, some nomadic
Aleuts wander," he wrote. "They are both local Aleuts and Kodiak
Aleuts. They ran off in former times, and they attack young Aleuts
and try to lead them off to join the nomads as comrades."

An American scientist who visited with Father Innokentii
Shaishnikoff in the 1870s found the belief very much alive and credited
the Outside Men to bands of unchristian Aleuts. Verne Robinson's
first major case as deputy U.S. marshal was the investigation of a mur-
der and suicide caused by belief in Outside Men.

Henry Swanson: *Then there was Brother Boots and his son
Simeon. When the picker-uppers went to get them on Segula at the end
of fox-trapping season they had the door of their cabin nailed solid from*

*the inside. They were both dead in the house. They had been dead quite*
*a while. They left a note saying there was an Outside Man or something*
*on the island. Anyhow, they nailed the door shut, and he shot the boy*
*and then he shot himself. He was a nice guy. I didn't think he would do*
*anything like that, but that's what happened.*

A comfort with fatality characterized Henry's stories.

This then is the design of Sophie's best baskets: small patterns of
varied colors repeated in regular intervals across the surface of the
basket. She achieved designs in three ways: false embroidery with colored thread, solid bands of colored weft, and open work through
crossed warp or separated weft. Although Aleut weavers developed
more than sixteen stitch varieties, Sophie generally restricted her
work to three: plain double-twining, crossed warp, and three-weft
corner rows.

Cap this chapter with dancing, cover it with a decorative lid, with
Jenny Krukoff and Sergie Sovoroff dancing at the end of summer. But
this dance reminds me of another that Anfesia told me about one
afternoon.

"*Akaiya! Akaiya!*" Behold! Behold!

When hunters had been at sea a long time and finally sighted
land they would exclaim, "Akaiya! Akaiya!" Dancers would shout this,
turning their wrists as though they were rowing a skin boat. When
John Golodoff sang once in this way, all you could hear was his voice
and the shush, shush of the gut raincoat moving on itself. Once, as his
singing gained speed and his movements grew more and more agi-
tated, he asked someone to open a window. The crowd was locked in
place and again he broke from his chant asking to have a window
opened. No one moved until he stopped and got angry and then
someone rushed to a window and everybody laughed. They had
thought his requests were just parts of the song.

Jenny Krukoff happened to be staying at Unalaska when the sisterhood held a get-together party for the town. Also visiting from

Nikolski were Sergie and Agnes Sovoroff. They were renting a place while they worked at the crab cannery in Captain's Bay. Agnes was the daughter of the noted singer and dancer German Stepetin. She had moved to Nikolski in 1924 when she and Sergie were married.

Sergie was in his early sixties. With elegant white hair combed back, his twinkling eyes and ready smile, he was a man of consummate poise and skills. Renowned for his models of Aleut skin boats, he also made sea otter spears and models of wooden fox traps. He had carved many of the furnishings for the Nikolski church while trapping fox on uninhabited islands in the Central Aleutians.

During a pause in the regular dancing, space was cleared in the middle of the rec hall as Sergie and Jenny came forward. I cannot remember if they danced to a phonograph record or if someone sang, but they danced—an Aleut dance, someone said.

"It wasn't Aleut," Anfesia told me later. "It was Russian."

Whatever it was, the audience was transfixed as Jenny and Sergie danced erect, flowing towards each other, circling and backing away. Each twirled a silk scarf that billowed beside them, before them, as they stepped in and out of its liquid flow. The scarves circled them like birds.

# 6

# A Beginner's Basket

Although airplanes came to town only two or three times a week, visiting the post office was a daily ritual. Some days the plane got in late and mail wasn't sorted until the next morning. Some days the postmaster was a little tired or under the weather and saved the third-class mail for the following day. Some days a misdelivered letter got returned, and you found it waiting for you. Whatever the excuse, a trip to the post office was a chance to visit with someone.

I checked my mail one afternoon near the end of September 1965. Phil Tutiakoff was sorting outgoing letters when I walked in. He said he'd heard I was trying to learn to weave baskets from Sophie Pletnikoff.

"Trying is right," I said.

"*Tunux̂taada* is a bit hard to understand sometimes, I bet."

I nodded.

"Don't feel bad," he said. "She's damn hard to understand even in

Aleut—even by Aleuts! It doesn't matter what language she uses." He laughed and said, "She talks faster than anybody."

He offered to introduce me to his mother, Anfesia Shapsnikoff, an accomplished Attu weaver who had taught classes for the Kodiak Historical Society.

I had seen Mrs. Shapsnikoff, of course, and heard about her. I'd even said a fleeting hello once or twice. Encouraged enough by Phil's friendliness to ignore his mother's intimidating reputation, I accepted his invitation. On September 28, Phil took me to the house he and his brothers had constructed out of military buildings after the family returned from the evacuation to Southeast Alaska and found their own home destroyed by weather and looters. Rather than merely attaching two or three cabanas together as the military had done when they established New Town, Anfesia's sons had joined them, peaked the ends to provide an upstairs, and covered the structure with a new roof. Of all the post-war houses in town theirs looked the least like a refurbished military structure. While a woodstove did its best to heat the living room, a trusty oil stove burned perpetually in the kitchen. A teapot sat on one side, brewing its dark, thick concentrate, while a kettle hovered near boiling closer to the firebox.

A gray-haired, hunch-backed woman scarcely taller than my elbows turned away from the stove as we came in. Her bright, dark eyes and sparrow-like stance were complemented by the clear soprano with which she greeted us. After laying a large spoon aside and drying her hands on a towel, she extended a hand, fine avian bones, and said, "I'm pleased to meet you—finally!" Phil and I sat at her table while she poured us all cups of tea and added a few fresh slices to the homemade bread already on a plate. She moved a can of butter and the sugar bowl closer to me. Phil explained what she already knew.

Anfesia Shapsnikoff agreed to try me as a student if I promised to write down what she said. She remarked that she'd had men as students before and mentioned a Baptist minister at Kodiak who had attended her classes. She invited me for tea after school. After a couple of visits she scolded me, lazy *Amirkaanchin*, when I confessed to not writing down her comments.

And so I wrote: *Unalaska weaving is done with the two weft strands on the outside of the woven basket. The grain of the woven stitches runs up and down the basket. Attu weaving is done with one weft inside the basket, twined around the fingers, and the other weft on the outside. These two are exchanged during the weaving of a stitch. The grain on Attu baskets tends to slant across the basket.*

*When weaving with grass it is necessary to dip your fingers into water and moisten the grass to keep it pliable.*

*She showed me a pattern of diamonds with dots inside that she said dated from 1842.*

*Grass from Atka is stronger and whiter than Unalaska grass. Attu grass is even stronger. She has some grass over thirty years old that is still good for weaving.*

Over a month passed from the time I met her until she began to give me direct instruction. First I had to begin learning how to harvest and prepare grass, although the entire process would take several months. Once the grass was ready it had to be graded and split into usable fibers. Then weaving could begin. She preferred to have beginners use grass weft strands, but she said I should continue with the raffia basket Sophie had started for me. "Chinamen's grass" she said her aunt had called raffia back around 1910 when the older woman was giving instruction to the girls at the school.

For my first trip to pick basket grass Anfesia suggested I go up the valley, just past the lake, where a crop of grass grew on the side of the hill. I found the spot above a small creek meandering down from Ski Bowl and crossing under a small bridge into the swampy flats leading to the lake. Knee-high blueberry bushes grew wherever the hillside slumped, but few berries were evident. Using my jackknife, I cut a large bundle of long thick stems with great waving blades of grass. The green was beginning to fade this late in September, but Anfesia had said the grass would still be usable. I questioned the need for all the long loose blade ends, so I cut them off and tied the thick stems into a firm bundle.

As I brought the grass into town, I met Mike Kudrin, Polly's father, carrying two full cans of blueberries. We walked together in silence until he turned to his home at the corner of New Town. When I walked into Anfesia's kitchen and handed her the truncated bundle, she burst out laughing.

Four days later I went out again, and this time I didn't cut off the blades. She had me put the grass in deep weeds and cover the bundle with a burlap sack. On October 10, I rinsed the grass in the bay and set the bundle in the shade. I went to the west side of the lake and picked some very long grass growing in a small cove. This I stashed among the high weeds just back from the lake. On the way home I climbed up toward the tidal wave houses and picked what was growing in a gully between the houses and the Ski Bowl road. I brought this down into town and laid it behind the shed, again covering it with burlap.

On October 15, snow fell all day, burying the grass. In the evening I shook the blades free of snow and rinsed them in salt water at the front beach. The grass floated gently in the water, and I quickly pushed on the blades, giving them a thorough dunking but catching them before a stronger wave sent them surging beyond my reach. I brought the grass back up and buried the bundles in snow.

Sophie had started my basket by twisting a weft strand around four or five warp strands and then gradually twining around each of the warp in turn and pressing them into a circular shape. This created a solid start to the basket but tended to make a rather coarse and lumpy beginning. Anfesia's method began with just two strands of grass.

*November 1, 1965. Beginning a basket. Start with two long weft strands. Loop them over each other and twine the one weft once over the other one. Hold this very tightly between the thumb and forefinger in the left hand. Place one new warp strand between the weft and twine over it. Add, one at a time, three more warp strands, twining over each of them in turn. Do not attempt to secure the short ends which are pointing down under the basket. Be certain to keep the work tight.*

*Having added the first four warp, now secure the short ends of
these warp by holding them between the back of the forefinger and
front of the second finger. This will keep them from moving around.
Now add and twine over warp No. 5. Then bring warp No. 1 back into
position and twine over it again; then add and twine over warp 6; then
warp 2, add warp 7, warp 3, add warp 8, and weave over warp 4. Be
sure to turn your work as you add the new warp and as you bring
around warp 1 through 4. You do this so the work doesn't bunch up. Do
not secure the ends, as this will cause a bulge at the center of the
bottom. Later warp will be secured, but not these initial few.*

*After weaving four or five rounds and adding warp on a regular
basis, the ends of new warp can be secured by weaving them in with the
following (old) warp.*

*The end tips then need to be bypassed on the next round of weaving
and tucked under the basket. Mrs. Shapsnikoff said that in her mother's
work these tips were woven into the fabric of the basket, and the inside
of her baskets was almost as smooth as the outside.*

Back home I worked steadily at the basket bottom, twining a few
stitches and then adding a new weave, twining a few more and then
adding. I spent two hours weaving and then took my work back to
Anfesia. She looked at it and quietly proceeded to rip out all I had
done, removing any intimations I might have had that learning basketry
was somehow a transcendental experience. It was nothing but work.

"You have to add these weaves on a regular basis!" she scolded.
Ruthless, I thought—and remembered how someone had lashed out
privately to me at what he viewed as Anfesia's capricious exercise of
power.

"If you don't add regularly, your work will be lopsided."

I began again.

I had known demanding teachers before. When I was sixteen my
parents agreed to pay for piano lessons if I bought a piano. I found
one I could afford at Horse Trader Harry's Used Car Lot. I had an

excellent teacher, Mrs. Delferna Berg, but soon the woman from whom she took lessons had scarfed me up. Although the change was approved by Mrs. Berg, my mother raised her eyebrows and never quite knew what to make of the eccentricities of Mildred Charlton-Hardy-Coleman. Through four years of Dohnanyi, Bach, and Bartok (and almost as many husbands), she tried to get me to understand that life and music energized each other.

"You don't study fencing," she quoted repeatedly, "to learn how to fence." She was appalled, I think, by my emotional lassitude, by the narrow frame in which I bound myself. She did two things for which I have always been grateful. One winter afternoon she drove me, her daughter, and Mrs. Berg from Yakima to Seattle where we met my Aunt Annie and heard Rubinstein give an all-Chopin recital. It was the first concert I ever attended. After dragging us backstage to shake Rubinstein's hand, she took us to a bar (scandalizing Aunt Annie) to listen to a jazz pianist. Anita and I were underage and had to sit out front in the restaurant. A year later she introduced me to the Latvian composer Volfgangs Darzins and arranged for me to have a lesson from him. He died the next summer. I remember him standing on the front porch of his small house near Green Lake, Seattle, the light coming down to his shoulders.

Now here I was, at some green corner of the world, taking lessons once again from another woman of remarkable mind and talent.

While I sat on Anfesia's couch one afternoon, still weaving away on my basket bottom, Phil walked through the door with a photographer from a national magazine. His jacket and vest creaked with notebooks and camera supplies, and he gave a confiding smile when he saw weaving going on. As he bent over and spread out his equipment he told Anfesia he would like to photograph her weaving a basket. With the fury of a williwaw lifting the surface of the bay, invectives and gestures swept across him as she ordered him off her property. He wrenched himself up, embraced his dangling cameras, meters, tripod, and film, and hurled off the porch. Later, with Phil's intercession and having made an appointment, he returned, cameraless, to discuss the possibility of photographing her.

It was while having tea at Anfesia Shapsnikoff's that, after practicing rudimentary sentences, I first spontaneously understood words in the Aleut language. By this time I had learned not to knock as I opened the outer back door and stepped into her storeroom. Tapping on the inner door at the same time I opened it, I greeted her. She welcomed me in, gestured to a chair at the table as she got a cup from the cupboard. She poured a little concentrated tea into the cup from a teapot on the oil stove and then filled the cup with boiling water.

"You know Mrs. Moller?"

"Yes. Hello." I smiled at the stern woman seated at the table and she nodded back.

"*Aang, aang.*" She was always Mrs. Moller. I think even God called her Mrs. Moller. She was a niece of Sophie Pletnikoff and Dora Kudrin.

We drank tea quietly. Learning silence was difficult for me to do (or not do, as the case might be) and I often failed. That day I ventured several comments that fell off the table. Mrs. Moller drank her tea. Anfesia played solitaire. When I again started talking Mrs. Moller placed her tea cup in the saucer and made a little noise at which Anfesia looked up. She spoke directly to Anfesia in Aleut. With a shock I understood as she asked, "What's he doing here? Why doesn't he leave?"

As I grew to know Mrs. Moller I saw her as a remarkable woman, astute and generous. I rarely visited her home without carrying away fresh *alaadiks*, a small jar of homemade jam, or a few pieces of smoked salmon. I never visited without having tea. But knowing her took time; she had no time for transients.

Eventually I noticed that my weft strands—in addition to getting brown from my dirty fingers—were growing dangerously short.

*November 18, 1965. Adding new weft strands. Twine a stitch and then bring over the next warp. The weft to be replaced (A) must now be the top one. Place the new weft (C) beside the warp and hold the end of the new weft (C) between the back of the forefinger and the front of the second finger. Twine a stitch over the warp and the new weft. The weft to be replaced (A) is now the bottom one and the other old weft (B) is on the top. Bring the short end of the new weft under the old weft (A) and lay it next to it. Bring over another warp. Now securely holding the warp, the old weft (A) and the short end of the new weft (C) between the thumb and forefinger of the left hand, bring the long end of the new weft (C) under these and twine a stitch using weft C and weft B. Thus the new weft's end is secured, and on the next round this end and the old weft may be tucked under the basket and woven in or cut off.*

The grass I had picked had now blanched to a deep yellow. In fact, some of it had spoiled and turned black and slimy. I placed the huge bundle on Anfesia's table, which she had cleared off. She began separating each stalk into individual blades, throwing the coarser outer blades on the floor and placing each of the inner three blades in distinct piles. She was especially careful with the very white, very tender, inner blades. Once we had separated all the stalks we carried out the discarded grass—by far the largest pile—and made sure that any slugs also were carried outside. She swept the floor and wiped off the table.

The three piles of grass—firsts, seconds, and thirds—were now to be strung in three distinct ways. The blades in each pile were sorted according to length by holding the pile vertically and tapping it on the table so all blades fell evenly to one end. The tips of the top blades were pinched together and lifted out of the pile. This process was repeated producing small bundles of grass in diminishing sizes. A long fine thread was twined over three or four inner blades at a time until all the blades were strung together. The thread was twined back, resulting in a double twined row. The string was tied in a knot when the beginning was again reached.

The seconds also were twined, but with this difference: After twining three or four blades together, another small bundle of three or four was placed in position to be twined. Now the tips of the first twined bundle were bent over and placed next to the new bundle and the twining commenced. The result was that the tips of the first bundle were secured against the sides of the second bundle. This process was continued to the end of the row when the twining strings were tied. Occasionally, but not often, this string of grass was secured with a second row of twining.

The thirds were coarser and longer blades and they were strung together by braiding their tips together. About six blades were tied some four inches from the slender tip of the grass. These blades were braided (three-strand braiding) for a few stitches. Then, a new bundle of three or four blades was added and braided over, the tips becoming part of one of the braiding groups. Now with every braid on the right a new bundle of blades was added so that the long blades began to hang down something like a skirt as the braid continued along. As the very tips of blades were reached in the braid they were dropped out; there were always plenty of newer ones with which to continue. When the last bundle had been incorporated into the chain, the braid was continued down the narrowing ends of grass and finally secured with a knot.

With all three of these methods, the grass could be hung outside on nails along the house or shed or on the clothes line. The grass could dry slowly, with air circulating around each blade.

The school year was going well. I still hadn't found a curriculum, but I had some notion about the destination we should be heading toward. Although I had been the only returning teacher, I declined the position of head teacher. The city clerk's job provided enough paperwork. Two teachers flipped a coin and Wilburta McGlashan, a woman with a kind but redoubtable heart, either won or lost: She got the position.

Carl Moses of King Cove had bought the store and property belonging to the Northern Commercial Company. The line of ownership for that tract of land extending from the church to the dock stretched back through the Alaska Commercial Company to the original Russian American Company. Walt and Marie Berthelsen ran the store for Carl. Walt had been in and out of the Aleutians for decades and Marie was originally from an Aleut village near the Alaska Peninsula. Carl sold the dock and some land to Pan Alaska Fisheries, who then burned the old warehouses dating back to the 1870s, warehouses filled with the account records and log books of the A.C. Company, with skin boat frames and other useless memorabilia. The Company House of the A.C. Company still stood, three stories of gradually crumbling splendor. The old store building continued to be used. The cannons that had surrounded the flagpole in the small yard in front of the store had vanished along with the flagpole.

The former Bureau of Indian Affairs hospital caught fire and burned. It had been repaired after damage during the 1942 bombing, and Pan Alaska was using it as a bunkhouse. After the volunteer fire department stretched out the firehose, hooked it to a hydrant, and turned the water on, the hose sprouted water along its length like a yard sprinkler. Old George Semple delivered more water with his garden hose.

I was drinking tea at Anfesia's one afternoon when Jenny Krukoff was visiting. Although she lived at Nikolski village, Jenny had been born on Attu Island. When I write about Jenny a melody goes through my head from a song Anfesia sometimes sang. Jenny's mother was an old blind woman from Attu and she would sing this lilting lament:

*Why are you crying?*
*I don't want you to be crying.*
*I didn't give you away to be married*
*so that you would be crying.*
*So don't be crying.*
*When I think of you I am always remembering*
*so be happy, don't be crying.*
*I will never forget you.*

Henry Swanson recalled once: *One time two old-timers came up to Commissioner Bolshannin's. One of them was Innokentii Petikoff. He was a real old-timer; in fact, he was old enough so that he was in Sitka when the U.S. bought Alaska. Well, him and that other old-timer brought a boy and girl to Bolshannin to get married. I was there and Bolshannin was looking for his book to read the marriage thing out of. He couldn't find it so he asked me if I would run up to Dr. Newhall's and get his book. So I started out and this kid came after me.*

*"Hey, you better stay back there," I said.*

*He said, "Ah, I don't want to get married. They're dragging me there to get married."*

*They used to do that. I remember this one time a man, I think his name was Krukoff, from Nikolski, went looking for a wife for his son. He went all over. He went to the Pribilofs and down to Unga and Sand Point, all over. He didn't get any and finally he took Jenny. You know, she was from Attu and she was here and he took her and they used her for a slave down there. There was the old man and his three or four sons living in that house and this Jenny was the servant.*

Jenny had been a widow for some years when she came to Unalaska. She was a superb weaver whose baskets combined an extraordinary fineness and evenness of weave with a dearth of decoration. I have seen one basket she wove that was entirely devoid of design. That afternoon at Anfesia's I watched while she diffidently lifted Anfesia's weaving from the table, wove a few stitches, and set it back down.

More tea was drunk. Anfesia and Jenny spoke quietly in Aleut, and Anfesia told me she was asking her what old-time Aleuts had used for wicks in their stone lamps.

Jenny wasn't saying. Anfesia picked up her basket and began weaving. This simple exchange commanded mastery. Jenny's actions complemented Anfesia on her work while quietly revealing her own skill. The act could be unnerving when a weaver had spent literally dozens of hours on a small basket and another person put her hands to it. Fingers that were slightly dirty would permanently stain the weft. Stitches with tension too tight would warp the sides. Stitches too loose would create an area swollen slightly from the uniform sides. If Anfesia had ripped out Jenny's stitches she would have offended her guest. By continuing her weaving she affirmed her visitor's skill.

When Sophie came to visit her, Anfesia hid her baskets.

In early December I stopped at Anfesia's one afternoon to see if she had learned from Jenny Krukoff the proper way to collect grass in late fall or winter. Jenny herself was there, and after I told Anfesia I'd come to see whether I should go after some more grass, she looked at Jenny and said, "You should take her with you." Then speaking in Aleut she arranged it and Jenny left to get her rain gear, as it was cloudy and misty out.

We crossed the creek and walked towards Haystack, climbing the flat knoll between the road and the reservoir. The grass was not abundant, but we found two clumps from which we each cut an armful. The grass was the same except now it had turned light yellow with white ends. The inner blades, which would be very short in this late grass, apparently weren't used as we cut the grass near the top of the stalk, where the wide outer blades branched out from the stem. She tied the bundles with three twisted blades of grass.

Mine she tied with a regular knot, but on hers she wrapped the narrow twisted ends around the stalk ends three times and tucked them under. This created a slip knot around the stem, and she pushed the twisted curls down the stalk to create a tight bond. Jenny said to show the grass to Anfesia, and she would tell me what to do with it.

Because Sophie Pletnikoff was Mrs. Moller's aunt, when I saw Mrs. Moller at her home or at Anfesia's, she invariably teased me.

"I saw you going to my aunty's! What were you doing, always going there?"

Anfesia would chime in, "Too many girlfriends!"

I think Sophie was relieved when Anfesia began giving me

lessons. While Anfesia never directly criticized Sophie's work, she let me know that Sophie was an Unalaska weaver and that the best weavers were from Atka and Attu. Sophie continued to welcome my visits—especially if I expressed interest in purchasing a doll or basket.

One afternoon Anfesia took a portion of some grass she had received from Atka and rolled a newspaper around it. She asked me to take it to Sophie.

No one answered when I knocked on Sophie's inside door. As I walked beside Dora Kudrin's house on my way out of New Town, a tapping at her kitchen window got my attention. Sophie beckoned me in to join her and her sister for tea. When Sophie unrolled the newspaper on Dora's kitchen table she exclaimed, "Ah, Aleut grasses!" This was a gift both pleasing and valuable.

I completed my first basket on January 24, 1966, and began weaving the cover. Four months later I had reached the outer edge of the cover and began turning the corner. On June 2, I was again at Anfesia's. That morning Mrs. Moller had brought her the first seagull eggs of the season, and she had made a custard of incredible richness. She had me taste it along with some seal meat Mary Robinson had given her the day before.

I made the final stitches securing the edge of the cover's lip. Anfesia clipped away the remnants of the warp. She placed the cover on the basket. It sat on her table, a worn-looking specimen whose fine top contrasted with a body that bulged with uneven stitches and a labored design. But it was finished.

"*Sanakux̂,*" she said.

I could start again.

# 7

# Approaching Small Bay

I cannot remember if it was summer or early fall. It wasn't spring, because in spring there is always snow that high in the mountains, and there was only a rock bridge dipping between two peaks like a weakened roof. From where I stood the bridge extended westward for two hundred feet, the slopes angling down evenly on each side about thirty feet where they were engulfed in fog.

Solid on the south, on the north the fog dissipated, shredded like the knees of old jeans, a glimpse of mountain flesh beneath. The western rise of this natural trail seemed to lead immediately onto a wide summit from which I expected to find my way back to town. Now even if the fog rose again I knew where to go. I took off my day pack and sat down.

I remembered Anfesia's admonitions against hiking alone.

Earlier that day I had left town and walked to Ugadaga Bay. Continuing southwest and toward the head of Beaver Inlet, I planned to explore the bay between Ugadaga and Uniktali, appropriately named Small Bay. To avoid the endless repetitions of bluffs and rocky beaches I had climbed onto the slopes circumscribing the inlet. Before I sighted the bay, the weather began closing in. I had reached a natural contour on the side of the hill and so continued gradually gaining altitude as visibility declined from about the length of a football field to its width.

Soon I was walking in an enclosure the size of a baseball diamond but even this was being lapped away by thickening clouds. I decided that if visibility shrank to the size of my school classroom I'd begin a gradual descent back toward the point of Ugadaga. If it shrank to a closet, I'd sit down and wait for a change.

Fog-walking utilizes ordinarily uncalled-on senses. The smell of the island's interior is lighter than the salt- and kelp-weighted sea air. Approaching water a hiker hears it shove and push against the shore, feels the weight of its fall against the beach. I walked slower. I memorized the order of plants as I passed them.

After two years in the Aleutians even this circumscribed environment was filled with familiar growth. I was no botanist and so this plant, nameless except to call it a thin grass, like the hair on my arms, had been used in basketry by Anfesia's aunt, the great weaver Maggie Prokopeuff of Attu. She picked it late in the fall and used it in her finest work. And this plant, three soft dark green toothed leaves on branching stems, was *petruskii*, suffused with a rich parsley flavor. I walked around a larger, greener, shinier plant aping the *petruskii*. This was "strong *putchkii*" whose leaves and stems produced burns on bare arms or hands, but whose medicinal roots were split, wrapped in cloth, and used as a poultice.

Behind me, closer to the shore, I had passed a scattering of Kamchatka lilies with their rice-like roots. And here was that plant I had first tasted with trepidation. It looked too much like the poisonous water hemlock of the Northwest to be eaten, but Anfesia had nibbled on it to relieve her sore throat.

After talking with Sergie Sovoroff of Nikolski one afternoon about Aleut names for plants, I took some comfort in my botanical ignorance. I showed him a white flower and asked him its Aleut name. He told me and he gave me the name of a yellow flower I handed him. Later I learned the names meant "white flower" and "yellow flower"! But Sergie knew that the leaves of this plant relieved intestinal pains and the roots of that flower were hallucinogenic. The names he gave were descriptive of those plants. Other names included "house of the bumblebee," for the monkshood where those bees loved to root for pollen; "scissors plant" for the iris whose petals resembled closed scissors. And there was a plant whose white blossoms were like seagulls.

I was beginning to define myself within a society of known plants, plants known to a people of a particular place, defining myself by where I was.

My route continued upward through surreal architecture. Fog-chilled now, I zipped my jacket, kept my hands in my pockets. Looking up I thought I glimpsed a rocky crest just as the walls of fog narrowed and I walked into the closet I'd been dreading. I laid my folded poncho on the damp ground cover and sat down. A few clumps of Maggie Prokopeuff's grass were growing within reach. As I began twining them into a small coarse basket bottom I knew that when the green blades dried the stitches would unravel. But as they did their dance between my fingers, perhaps this was prayer, perhaps this was meditation.

The only experience I had ever had that might be called religious involved those two words, prayer and meditation, words I never understood. Ten years before I had sat in confirmation robes with my class of young Lutherans. For two years we had memorized the catechism, and the short explanation of the catechism, and now we'd been examined by members of the church. The examination, never intended to embarrass or assure anyone, had passed quickly and we were admitted to our first communion, believing the body and blood of Christ were present among us. Believing that, I had no trouble believing the words in the Bhagavad-Gita and in the Tao Te Ching possessed as much validity as those of Moses or Luther. But when I raised that question, I was told that since they'd passed uncommented upon in either the Old or New Testaments, they were without foundation, better forgotten or ignored. Good thinkers, certainly, and probably kind, but having nothing to do with salvation or the brotherhood of Christ.

I realize if I had had an ecumenical Christian guide I might have reconciled these corners of the world, as there was much about the church I loved. But as it happened I met a Bahá'í and began attending "firesides" at his home. Although he and his wife had several translations of Bahá'u'lláh's works, they tended to give me talks and explanations his son 'Abdu'l-Bahá (1844-1921) delivered during his visits to Europe and the United States from 1910 to 1912. It all seemed so reasonable. The independent investigation of truth. The unknowable essence of God. The harmony of science and religion. Such nice people. The equality of women and men. An international auxiliary language. Such delicious cookies. A spiritual solution to the economic problem. The Most Great Peace.

One night, against the advice of my hosts who thought the book too difficult, I insisted on borrowing the *Kitab-i-Iqan*, Bahá'u'lláh's *Book of Certitude*. Written in two days in 1862 in response to questions from a learned Moslem, it unfolded an account of progressive revelation for me like a broad and complex fugue. I knew now where I stood, where my beginnings were. Shortly after reading this book I became a Bahá'í, and my father said, "If you can't believe in your own religion, I don't see how you can believe in someone else's." And then a visiting Bahá'í woman, disparaging my major when she learned I was studying philosophy, remarked, "But how can you? Knowing what you know?"

Philosophy and poetry and prayer. I had little success balancing the rigorous demands of epistemological proofs with poems that released an immediacy of knowledge measured as much by blood and androgynous lust as by metered sound and rhyme. And this religion I had signed up with made so many demands: no premarital sex, no alcohol, no drugs, no affiliation with political parties; obligatory prayer, a calendar of feasts and holy days, a fast.

A Tlingit man and a Yup'ik woman taught me some modesty—or gave it a good try. Eugene and Melba King lived near the university, and I would visit them and read their mail while Melba fretted about the lights. Both of them were blind. Their house was comfortably bare. A few bas-relief carvings hung on the walls. Some lace doilies were pinned to the arms and back of the davenport.

Melba had been blind since birth, a master of Braille, an astute administrator, a secretary for a local firm. In 1943 she had become the first Bahá'í of Inuit heritage. Eugene had gone blind later in life and, unlike Melba, who had a seeing eye dog, used a white cane and seemed more bounded by his loss of sight. He reached the root of any question I had and valued its worth whether or not he had an answer. He restored balance with his laughter. Tlingit culture, remembered, dynamic, and enduring, framed his remarkable mind. He measured what he said. Melba was all love and practicality.

In the turmoil of that year, I had a dream. I did not believe in dreams. 'Abdu'l-Bahá paced across a white room: a carpet on the floor, a lamp, an overstuffed chair, a bookcase filled with books. I don't know—I never recalled—what was said, but only that we talked a long, long time. I remembered sitting on the floor, then standing behind him, relaxing in the chair. Finally I'd had enough and opened up the glass doors on the bookcase and took out a book. I thumbed through it at random, anything for distraction, to avoid whatever we were discussing. Then he took out two large white volumes and put them in my lap. They were written in a script I didn't know, a script with swirls and circles.

"I can't read this," I said.

And then I heard his voice behind me, through the night's dream and into morning as I awakened. I lay in bed, eyes shut but certainly awake, and heard repeatedly what he'd said: pray and meditate, pray and meditate. All day I could recall the timbre of that voice, the quality and tone. Then I could feel it dissolving out of experience and into memory, where it stayed.

I did not believe in dreams. I knew that only reason could resolve difficulties with certainty. Yet here had been this dream as real as any waking moments. I never knew what to do with it. I never knew how to pray or meditate. I read the prayers and meditations of Bahá'u'lláh, but I also read his admonitions that an hour's reflection was preferable to seventy years of pious worship, that work done in the spirit of service was worship.

Perhaps the things we do are prayers; the things we see, our meditations?

I'd been sitting for fifteen or twenty minutes, enough to get thoroughly chilled. I figured I'd have to move soon. A light ceiling appeared suggesting the fog was thinner higher up. I'd go slowly. I'd go carefully. I tossed the woven fragment back into the grass and started up.

The light increased in brightness. The clouds around me thinned as I neared the top. I came out at the eastern end of a rock bridge. I turned around and sat facing Beaver Inlet. The fog covered my side of the inlet, fringed a bit towards Ugadaga Bay. From the water's center to the far mountains on the opposite side, it was clear. I looked eastward toward Biorka, where there were no lights at evening, where the graves went untended, a place people still called home or more often these days, a place people could call my mother's home, my father's home.

I had by now taken my first- and second-graders, including grandchildren of some Biorka people, to cut basket grass. We had gone out one afternoon to the side of the lake where the grass grew up through a growth of ferns. We cut grass and picked berries. We ate the berries and brought the grass back to school where we wrapped it in burlap and set it beside the building.

Although the villages in Beaver Inlet were distinct settlements they formed an interrelated whole—an inlet community. Nick Galaktionoff, Sr., was the father of two of my students. He is today an Unangan treasure. Through him—from Andrew Makarin, Alec Ermeloff, and other men of Biorka—comes a line of memory extending to the time the villages of Beaver Inlet were complete. The chief of the largest village, on the eastern end of the inlet, was paramount and, at least as contained in Nick's oral history, he jealously guarded the resources of the area. Subordinate villages survived at his pleasure.

So much about this society is speculation; their detailed complex art is certain: carved ivory and bone, bent and painted wood; woven grass; sewn, embroidered, and appliquéd gut and skin. Each of these arts or crafts was highly developed.

Their basketry contained a profusion of stitches. The basic stitch was plain twining with two weft strands. When both strands were natural grass, the even surface of most basketry occurred. When one or both the wefts were colored, however, a variety of running patterns resulted. Bands of this sort are on the oldest fragments recovered from burial caves on the Islands of Four Mountains and on the southern end of Unalaska. Plain twining was also done over divided warp, creating triangular interstices on large utilitarian baskets. This stitch was sometimes "driven home" so that the finished work appeared like regular, if slightly coarser, weaving—but of unusual strength.

For decorative rows of open work, the twining was sometimes done over crossed warp that kept its vertical lines or extended diagonally across the patterned rows. On rare baskets, this weaving was done over warp that crossed two lines and produced a more complex-appearing stitch.

Occasionally a weaver combined techniques, interrupted rows of plain, open weaving with a pattern of diverted warp or added an additional warp and carried it along on top, or twisted pairs of warp in slender lines. In these mats or baskets, the designs were subtle, slight variations in the weaving's regular pulse.

Weavers never seemed to tire of using a variety of stitches. Occasionally regular plaiting (over and under, over and under) was done with a colored strand of fiber, some dark root, dyed gut, or bright yarn. Very rare work shows wrapped, twined weaving and designs achieved by the deliberate introduction of a third weft strand to make a pattern out of slightly longer stitches.

The only variation that I used was crossed warp for a row or two of open work. Sara, Helen Merculieff's daughter, showed me a basket made completely with this stitch. She laughed and said it was a mistake. The weaver had misunderstood when Sara had asked for some open work showing and she had woven the entire lacy basket that way.

I crossed the bridge and started down Raven's Roost. The mountains kept the fog on the Beaver Inlet side of the island and the way home was clear. I skirted a small valley, its glacial lake banked against a cliff. A protective anonymity had kept it nameless. Like many other places on the island, this valley had no name and would have none, say what they would those cataloging hags who came periodically to survey for the state or town. Once named, soon altered: a trail, an access road, a sign.

Nearing the bottom of the road, at the head of the valley, I found a growth of basket grass. The blades weren't long, but they were wide and flaked with white spots. Anfesia had said a grass like this was favored at Atka. When I reached town and looked behind me, I saw clouds now banked above the Ugadaga pass while a tongue of fog licked the shoulder of Raven's Roost. Anfesia was home when I laid the grass inside her back porch and knocked on the inner door.

I had learned how great it was to be a stranger, to be welcomed at tea where languages meet, to be present where words, kind emissaries in this time of urban nomads, come out to say come in, sit down, have tea. She gave me tea, suggesting a way of being in this world I had not thought possible. I finished my tea and took the cup to the sink. I said good-night. She thanked me again for the grass. She closed the door behind me.

The foggy breath from Beaver Inlet filled the town.

8

# A Winter Hike

A storm was imminent when seagulls rose in elevated spirals over the shore, tilting avian crescents warning us to get ready for a good blow.

The botanist Eric Hulten wrote, "It is quite clear that the mosaic of plant communities in the Aleutians is to a large extent regulated by the wind." Veniaminov was more emphatic: " . . . one can say with certainty, that [above all] the local climate depends entirely upon the winds."

Winter starts in October and lasts through April. Spring's first impatient blossoms can be smothered by snow in May. But seven months of winter is enough; out of sheer stubbornness, and however contrary to appearances, May is the beginning of spring.

Any account of Aleut weather divination may be like the reconstruction of Aleut dance, and owe more to contemporary imagination than to continuous tradition. Although sources are scant—ethnographic accounts and fortuitous tourist films—still dance may be reassembled with some claim to authenticity. However, I know of no visitors to the Chain or contemporary residents who stood long enough, morning after morning, days into weeks, with the old men in the lee of a building to learn what they were observing.

Veniaminov, alone once again among ethnographers, learned that "high clouds moving in opposite directions from lower ones presage prolonged winds." The density and duration of January fogs foretold the extent of March snowstorms. Continuous frosts from the end of December through January were a prelude to warm weather in April and May. A bad spring produced a good summer and fall. However, he wrote nothing about seagulls.

Whatever signs Aleuts gathered and compiled (with as much art as science) resulted in accurate predictions in a land of constant weather flux.

"I always tell people the weather is going to be bad," said Henry Swanson, explaining his reputation as a forecaster, "so they think I'm a good weather prophet. Once in a while I tell them it's going to be good, you know, and it's not good. But if you tell them it's going to be bad, you'll be right most of the time."

Despite Henry's denigrations, there were signs that could be read, although elders in Veniaminov's time were emphatic about the gradual worsening of weather over recent generations. Hilda Berikoff's husband, Bill, found that his arthritic aches announced changes in the weather. He was the son of Emilian Berikoff, a noted sea otter hunter from the turn of the century. I never learned whether or not Bill attributed his condition to a violation of traditions as John Gordeiff had. Anfesia Shapsnikoff told me that Charlie Hope dug up a bone figure in his yard and when John Gordeiff saw it, he recognized it as an old-time amulet. He said he was so crippled with arthritis—his hands doubled into fists—because of the way his grandparents had treated amulets. How you treat them, he had told her, is how you will be.

Storms at Unalaska generally came from southeast, due north, or southwest. Storms from the southeast arrived throughout the year: avalanche of rain, houses sucking rain into their pores, exhilaration of horizontal rain. Calm often by morning. Again, Veniaminov: "... in 1833, on March 17th, there blew from the SE such a wind that it was literally impossible to keep on one's feet. It blew with equal force and the same direction throughout the entire local district."

Storms out of the north were most severe in the winter and especially during high tides: three days, five days, seven days. Cold eventually boring through wood, piercing the oil stove. Snow blowing into shoulder-high banks. The road along the shore littered with driftwood and debris. Anfesia's diary entry for December 12, 1968, noted one of the harsh complications brought by such storms: "Blowed all nite. Stove went out at 8:14 A.M." When a stove went out during a northern storm, it was often caused by water freezing in the oil line, and so one of her sons, Tracy, Tim, Phil, or Greg, would crawl under the house with a blowtorch looking first for elbows that might have frozen. If the line stayed frozen and the house cooled, the water lines could expand and break.

Fall southwestern storms hurled the most violent, mind-numbing winds. Heart-rupturing storms. The landscape altered. Houses nothing but sticks.

On October 5, 1880, Lucien McShane Turner experienced one of the vast Aleutian storms while at Attu, the most western of the islands. In his published weather observations, he noted:

> *A furious gale with gusts of a hurricane rate all day; the roof of my house was taken off, the boards loosened, a flood of water entered from the torrents of rain; the anemometer carried off and bent out of shape; all my specimens of natural history, including a complete series of plants from various islands of the Aleutian Chain were ruined; no help of any kind here and very little with which to repair damage; all records written in ink were in most instances hopelessly ruined; the wind blew . . . over the mountain tops in the most violent gusts.*

Some years later when writing his *Descriptive Catalogue of Ethnological Specimens*, Turner was in the middle of a sentence describing Aleutian coastlines when that October storm again burst into his brain. The result was a very terrible sentence, perhaps the worst ever written about the Aleutians, but one which inadvertently testifies to the enduring strength of Aleutian storms:

*The shores are mostly abrupt or precipitous, difficult of approach
except where the deeply indented coast has preserved the falling masses
of rock and stones rolled into shingle and boulders of all sizes by the
constant lashings of the sea waves impelled by the relentless fury of an
ever changing atmosphere producing violent storms of long duration
that cause the very foundations of the mountains to tremble under the
crushing impetuosity of the struggling billows of an ever angry ocean.*

In fairness to Turner it should be stated that the *Descriptive
Catalogue* exists only in a first-draft manuscript and was never polished for publication.

And Veniaminov again: "This region is the empire of the winds."

As a young man, the great chief of Unalaska, Alexei Yatchmenef,
was a member of a sea otter hunting expedition that was caught in a
storm at the end of summer in 1885. Terrible winds caused the deaths of
several of his companions and forced him and others ashore for several days. The ancient prohibition against grumbling about severe or
adverse winds is reflected in the restrained account he wrote in Aleut
in 1910. As translated by Knut Bergsland and Moses Dirks, his first comment on the weather was "A breeze from the northeast blowing up to
a storm, we passed four nights there." The gradual increase in winds
on this occasion confirmed Veniaminov's statement that winds which
began imperceptibly and grew gradually were the longest-lasting.
Yatchmenef continued, "The wind became strong, and in the evening
there came rain. . . . we lay down to sleep. . . , and, hearing the wind
and the rain sounding like singing, I spent the night without sleeping."

Just as wind regulated the growth of plants and shaped the
weather, so it colored every day in people's lives. Here at Agamgik Bay
on a calm morning in late October, a wet breeze off the bay. Logs ran-
domly jackknifed into the beach. The goddamned wind kept me up
most of the night. I thought the roof of the Quonset was going to get
torn off like the lid on the can of sardines I had eaten for supper. Near
morning the wind quieted and I fell asleep.

I had first found this Quonset on a Friday afternoon in early May. As soon as school ended that day I'd made a quick trip to the Alaska Communications System's office to make a telephone call on the only phone in town. Then I'd run home, thrown some food and clothes into a backpack, stopped at Anfesia's to tell her where I was headed, and made a quick three-hour hike to Agamgik.

The Quonset was the sole survivor of four ranged in a row behind the hill on the south side of the bay. Its north side was lashed to the hill with chicken wire and rags of disintegrating camouflaging. The south side was banked with grass and salmonberry bushes, although now by late October, the grass was bleached and bent upon itself, and salmonberry bushes were skeletal brambles. The doorless wall on the west end had two windows overlooking more salmonberry bushes, a quick drop down a narrow ravine, and the route down from the Humpy Cove pass. The east end was identical to the west except that it had a door. When I stumbled upon the cabin and climbed through the broken screen on the bottom half of this outside door, it looked like any abandoned Quonset: windows intact but clouded, the floor buckled. A shrunken fox carcass hung from a coat hook, still exuding the rancid oil that kept other fox and ground squirrels away. Then I noticed the back wall had a door. I untwisted the wire latch and stepped into a room that had obviously been lived in. There were two metal cots with mattresses rolled up. A table with benches, a small wooden stand, a sink that drained outside the wall, a makeshift "easy" chair, and in the center of the room, on a cement square raised on four white bricks, stood a wood-burning stove made from a fifty-gallon oil barrel. The stove pipe had rusted, but later I found enough extra pieces to patch it back together. Heavy white chipped crockery was on the table. The metal shelves on the side walls held a few decomposed packages of tea, a rusted tobacco can, an empty Vicks jar, some coiled string. Leaning against a wall were wooden implements I didn't recognize and later learned were fox stretchers and a tapered pole used in removing fat from the pelts.

After the war the Zaharoffs had erected the partition midway in this Quonset and established a fox trapping station. Their original cabin at Chaluuknax̂ had collapsed. The Agamgik station was not used for many seasons, however, as the price of fox had fallen to next to nothing.

There was a trail most of the way from Humpy Cove to Agamgik Bay. In fact, it began as a road among Quonsets at the east end of the Humpy Cove outpost. One Quonset, although it had no end walls, had a picnic table where I sometimes sat while the faded pinup girls glued to the walls gradually peeled away. Time's voyeur. The road quickly narrowed to a broad trail as it curved around a hill to where a footbridge had spanned a narrow canyon. The bridge had long since fallen into the gorge and so, after climbing down and up, I rejoined the trail as it followed the lowest terrain over the hills and petered out near a shallow pond at the summit. In the spring or after a week or two of heavy rain, a few ducks might pause there, but by the middle of summer the water had usually evaporated.

From the summit there were two routes I took on different occasions to Agamgik. On the first I continued straight ahead, maintaining the same elevation around the edge of the mountains. This route required descents and climbs, but the reward was a spectacular view of the bay and Beaver Inlet. The other, easier route wound down the hills, across a wide valley where it skirted a narrow stream, and around a lower hillside that gradually opened over the small peninsula that juts from the south side of the bay. This peninsula, backed by a small lagoon, formed the pebbled beach below the huts.

Once I'd located the Quonsets, Agamgik became my frequent destination. While blueberries and fish were scarce here, salmonberries banked the Quonset hut. In the spring I picked breakgreens, and late one fall I dug the roots of the stinky flower, the chocolate lily, the Kamchatka lily, resting beneath the fallen stars of their leaves. These roots were white bulbs surrounded by rice-like granules. Washed, cooked in shallow water covered with a *putchkii* leaf, the result was a pasty starch. Mix in some fish or a few of the blueberries and a good meal was ready. Perhaps not as good as boxed macaroni and cheese, but good to know about in any case.

The beach had agates, clear and clouded, fractured by constant tumbling in the surf, along with small pieces of red and green jasper. Soon the windowsills in the Quonset were lined with stones. I couldn't resist slipping a few stones into my pocket that October morning even though I'd gone to the beach to collect wood. I kept, whenever the waves were bountiful, a stock of driftwood in the outer room. Over weeks it would gradually dry and then it could be cut or chopped for the stove. To arrive at Agamgik and find all the dry wood burned and no reserve drying was to find my work tripled.

The night before I had found an old candle rolled in a piece of damp cloth and tucked into the back of a high metal shelf. With fresh candles I didn't need to burn this one, but I wanted to burn it, so I banked it with agates in the center of an overturned plate on a plastic Japanese crate near the cot.

While water heated for soup and tea, I started on a can of sardines, some cheese, and pilot bread. Perhaps it was because I was so desperate to pee that I imagined the wind was slackening. Outside the tin drum of the Quonset hut, the gusts seemed less ferocious with the whole world to contain them. As soon as I came inside the wind became steeper; the storm brought darkness early. I lit a candle on the table and a small sea of darkness formed below. The light above emphasized the angles the brown rectangular masonite panels formed as they leaned from the walls to the ceiling. After I finished the soup and rinsed out the pan, I brewed a cup of tea.

I crammed a few more chunks of wood into the stove, worried a little that the fire would get too hot for the thin sides of the old barrel. I took off my damp shirt and pants and draped them over the wire stretched near the stove. My long underwear had stayed dry so I slipped on a sweater, put the tea and the lit candle on a shelf near the head of the bed, and crawled into my sleeping bag. I dug away a small circle of wax around the blackened wick of the old candle and held it over the lit one. The wax edge melted and smoked before the wick ignited. I wedged the old candle into the cluster of agates and blew out the other.

The remnants of the past were part of what we were.

Fog had swallowed the village as I descended the school steps and started home. I could barely discern buildings a few yards away when I became aware of a movement and then of a shape deep in the murk. Seven- or eight-year-old John Moller, Mrs. Moller's grandson, dressed in miniature fatigues, was playing army with his plastic helmet and rifle. His size made him seem distant and for an instant, as he raced through high grass before the fog absorbed him, as he ran with an alert, defensive sweep beside a cabana, I felt the spectral reality of war with a jolt I never again experienced.

In 1982 and 1992 Unalaska hosted commemorations of the June 3 and 4, 1942, attack by Japanese forces on Dutch Harbor/Unalaska. On both occasions former servicemen returned and told about their experiences during the war. Compared with the earlier event, the commemoration on the fiftieth anniversary was larger, more intensive, better organized, and explained in far greater depth the contributions the U. S. military had made to the defense of Alaska. Yet as a local event, the 1982 commemoration had a defining act. This act, orchestrated by Phil Tutiakoff, was the dedication of a memorial stone by representatives of the American, Canadian, and Japanese armed forces and by representatives from the Aleut people. This ceremony, complete with Orthodox hymns, Japanese saki, and military pomp, lifted the commemoration out of memory and it became a part of our lives, as Aleuts from the evacuation mingled with veterans including Admiral James S. Russell and General Benjamin B. Talley of the United States, and Colonel Zenji Abe and Admiral Hiroichi Samejima from Japan.

But nothing anyone ever said, no photographs or films, no careful expositions of strategies and consequences, not even the symbolic and very real reconciliations of 1982, nothing ever made the war at Unalaska as real to me as it had seemed that instant John burst from the fog.

Who had left behind the old candle? Some luckless GI? One of the men who'd tried fox trapping after the war? And why was it rolled up inside a piece of cloth? To keep it from rats? Because it had been used on some special occasion in the church? Whomever it had belonged to, we now shared something. We shared this light.

The war in the Aleutians witnessed the capture of American territory and the imprisonment of civilians. Disembarking from their landing craft, five hundred Japanese troops waded ashore on Kiska Island on June 6, 1942. Soon they had captured the small U.S. Navy aerological unit stationed there. A day later Attu was taken and this secured the Japanese hold on the Western Aleutians. After living for three months in their occupied village, the forty-one Aleut residents of Attu were shipped to a detention camp in Otaru, Hokkaido, where they remained until the surviving twenty-five were liberated in 1945. The government schoolteacher was held elsewhere in Japan; her husband died during the initial capture of the island.

In May 1943, the battle of Attu climaxed a prolonged aerial bombing of the island from U.S. positions hastily erected on Amchitka and Adak. On May 11, 1943, in the aftermath of a storm, U.S. Army troops landed on Attu. However massed in numbers, however psyched for battle, the troops were crippled from the start. Paralysis of air support, rivalry in command, delayed supply routes, and ineffective communications compounded what the Aleutian spring did to men clothed for tropical warfare. Winds flayed those who advanced; cold froze the feet of those who waited. Casualties from weather—frostbite and trenchfoot—surpassed those wounded by enemy fire, 1,200 to 1,148. Five hundred forty-nine Americans were killed; 2,350 Japanese bodies were found. Twenty-nine Japanese survived as prisoners of war. The cost of routing the enemy on Attu was surpassed only by that on Iwo Jima.

For troops stationed on Umnak and Unalaska, the Japanese attack on the port of Unalaska was as far as enemy action went. After that, for them—and for the thousands who arrived later—their only enemy was the weather. Henry Swanson dropped off men to establish the outpost at Chaluuknax̂. Frozen snow buried the shoreline, obscured the contours of the hills. Unlike the men who landed on

Amchitka in January 1943, the men here found no Orthodox cemetery, no wooden crosses to dislodge and burn for campfires. They
returned to Dutch Harbor to wait for spring.

Surrounded by storm I blew out the candle and listened. The rain
that during the war had washed across this sheltered Quonset, struck
the rusted tin like shot. As it shook, if it stirred, if it breathed, I hoped
in twenty years the building had learned to lean a little closer to the
bank. The sound of wind was itself a physical presence, of a higher
pitch but of the same caliber as the growling swell that rode under-
ground before earthquakes. I knew how wind had shaped the island,
but now it seemed to be ripping the roof off the Quonset hut.

But in the morning loose camouflaging still hung from chicken
wire stretched across the roof. And the roof was still there. Rain had
varnished anything metal with a sheen of ice. Shocks of frozen grass
were clumped with snow.

With stones in my pockets and arms full of damp wood, I
climbed the slope from the beach back to the Quonset hut. The calm
was temporary, and if I delayed leaving I'd probably end up walking
for hours in foul weather. But then, the wind had finally come out of
the southeast, its most common direction. It had paused, and when it
resumed, it would probably be from the same direction and give me a
boost over the pass. But then again, if I stayed an extra day, who knew
what direction the wind would come from? The first snow had fallen
on the higher peaks a week ago and last night's snow had deepened it.
A north wind in late October could easily deliver a landscape of drifts
and whiteouts.

The morning air was so clear, the calm so complete, the stillness
so engulfing that I decided I'd explore the other Quonsets to see if
anything could be moved into the hut. I'd done this before and found
an immovable cast iron bathtub, an immovable huge metal sink and
drainboard, an unbudgable, vast kitchen cookstove. That morning I
uncovered a brass mushroom doorknob and then gave up scrounging.

The eastern end of the small bowl protecting the Quonsets rose to a plateau overlooking Beaver Inlet. An entrenched lookout shack provided a view of the inlet's mouth. Two men would have been a crowd in that cramped cave whose walls were slowly being squeezed in at the base. Crude pencil drawings of planes were on one wall. At the edge of the sloping hill there was a drop of about fifty feet to the water. A little south the bank became less precipitous and it was possible to reach the shore. From Agamgik to Chaluuknax̂ the coast was a series of pebbled beaches and abrupt outcroppings. Most of the rocky points were passable at all except the highest tides, when it was necessary to backtrack and climb over the grassy hillsides.

Midway between Agamgik and Chaluuknax̂, I descended to a beach heavily salted with agates. After pocketing a collection of rocks I started back, followed the contours of cliff edge over the brown, crumpled grass of October.

Across Agamgik Bay, at its northeast corner, Eagle Rock waded slightly off shore. A prominent bulky pinnacle that bore a faint resemblance to a seated eagle, the rock wore a green cap indicating it was a favorite perch for nesting or scouting birds. The base was cut in—Henry said it had been used for target practice by the big guns at Dutch Harbor during the war. Farther north, protected from guns by the curve of the coast, another pinnacle straddled the beach. Its steep front sank into the water. Its back swept to the hillside with a flowing cape. Rock shoulders and head, it was perhaps the petrified demon Veniaminov had written stood in this vicinity.

Snow ingots weighted the gray hills. A darkened red fox dropped below a bank as I approached the outskirts of Agamgik. The sky lowered over distant cliffs and squalls scratched at the inlet. I ran for the Quonset.

# 9

# Village Lives, Village Grief

Anfesia said to me one day, "I'll tell you an Aleut secret."

If you have patience.

If you will not rush to judgment.

People in the village mirrored the violence and destructive unpredictability of Aleutian weather. I remember women and men beaten unconscious by drunks, the victims often drunk themselves. The aged, absorbing the wounds of their adult children, became parents to their grandchildren. As best it could, the community protected children, but there were times when children were hungry and neglected. People lashed out with knives and fists and words while do-nothing gossips trailed skeins of half-truths.

No one with sense or compassion attempted to explain why

people drank. Explanations always posited simplistic solutions. The reasons for drinking were as varied as the reasons for not drinking.

I had a friend who cried when he was drunk and laughed hung-over. No matter how painful his mornings-after were, he did this again and again: he cried dead drunk and laughed hung-over. God grant me, I sometimes thought, such a resurrection.

But no violence exceeded that done by the state's salaried social worker who arrived in town armed with the blunt certitude of the law. Over fifteen months beginning the summer of 1967, she emptied the town of children. While I was on a visit to my parents, Anfesia wrote to me, "I have written Juneau and told them what is happening. . . . I let them know Unalaska could keep neglected children too like elsewhere so they could know of their Native ways, so Aleuts could be restored. . . ."

This dark was deeper than any storm. An Aleut proverb said the wind was not a river. Storms ended, but the repercussions from this act did not. But hope was a river, and among the twenty-two children scheduled for removal, one boy hid with friends until the social worker had ushered her bewildered cargo aboard the plane. His refusal to submit to authorities, his adept concealment, made him for that terrible week the last authentic asx̂aadax̂. Out of a sense of self-preservation, this child had revived an institution, but he was not the Outside Man against whom Andrew Makarin guarded the town by blessing its borders with holy water. Andrew had no power against the outside forces that assaulted the village. He exemplified the victimization against which Anfesia railed: "Things I heard of long ago are happening. Unknown people are coming, taking over our land and the things we made our living with. So let's get together and prevent these by speaking up."

Andrew was not weak. He was a man of exceptional resolve and courage. He had been part of the forced evacuation during World War II and returned to attempt re-establishment of Biorka village. The depletion of resources doomed his efforts. After living at Unalaska for several years he went one last time to Biorka and ceremonially burned the church, erecting a small wooden house over the spot where the altar had been. Nevertheless, by the time Dorothy M.

Jones, assisted by Father Gromoff, recorded an interview with Andrew, his voice had become a whisper. He seemed all bones and angles. And when, at Anfesia's suggestion, I visited Andrew one afternoon and asked about the Aleut language, the hand that had written in a firm script the entire Aleut text of Innokentii Shaishnikoff's 1861 *Short Rules for a Happy Life* drew two words for me: *Unangam aasmuka.* The words, *Aleut alphabet,* were enough to demonstrate a text.

Andrew: striding to church with his blind wife in tow. She was an accomplished seamstress who ran his house efficiently, but whenever they went out together, Andrew raced forward, dragging his petite wife like a kite on a short string.

Andrew: hunter, trapper, boatman for whom Beaver Inlet was home; telling Anfesia that wild onions could be smelled growing at English Bay; telling Nick Galaktionoff about Kiichxix̂ Kangax̂tax̂, the place where a braided rope of hair and grass had spanned the inlet.

When Sergie Sovoroff came to town from Nikolski to work in the crab cannery, he spent his evenings making models of *baidarkas,* Aleut skin boats (the *iqyax̂* and *ulux̂tax̂*). Sergie used yellow cedar for the runners, gunwales, ribs, and hatches, and gnarled joints of willow for the bow and stern. Yellow cedar, *lalux̂,* was prized for its strength and bendability; and of all wood that drifted ashore, it was the most valuable. The wooden frames were covered with cured fur seal throats that Sergie secured from the Pribilof seal harvests. His wife Agnes sewed gut raincoats to outfit the men Sergie placed in the *baidarkas* and wrote brief narratives in English to accompany each model. Sergie was literate, but only in Aleut. People spoke wistfully about sleeker, more detailed models once made by Alex Ermeloff and Andrew Makarin. Andrew had stopped making models when informed that if he earned money, the government check with which he helped his extended family would be cut off.

Andrew: resting in winter grass above the lake. Sending his daughter Irene for medicinal plants: *alix̂siisin, uulngiiĝdigan,* saxifrage and yarrow.

Andrew: patriarchal, aloof, on whom so many depended. In the absence of a priest, Andrew, Anfesia, and John Golodoff conducted services, officiated at funerals, and baptized infants.

Lay persons had been pivotal in the establishment of Christianity among Aleuts in the eighteenth and nineteenth centuries, and their roles in the church in the twentieth century were no less vital. In early summer 1963, Andrew became seriously ill and spent several months in Anchorage. He asked Anfesia to care for his wife during his absence, and she did so, buying food, taking her to a visiting doctor, and having her company at the fish camp at Devilfish Point.

In August, Bishop Amvrossy ordained John Golodoff as Psalmist. John had long been highly regarded for his work with the choir, and now he played an even greater role in services. Anfesia deferred to Andrew and John, but at times each of them was forced to read the service alone. When John died suddenly on Easter morning 1965, Andrew was again in Anchorage, and it fell to Anfesia to conduct the funeral service alone. A month later the former Father Nagosky, now Bishop Vladimir, visited Unalaska and held a memorial service for John. John's son, Ben, had been like another child in Anfesia's home and now as an adult he often extended her his help.

Although Andrew's health was poor, he baptized Gabriel Krukoff on May 13, 1965, and on November 14 he baptized his great-granddaughter in his home. Nevertheless, Anfesia was pleased when the bishop asked her son Phil to become a Reader. He held his first service on December 3 and assisted Andrew at Alex Berikoff's funeral at the end of the month.

On April 24, 1966, the Bishop of Alaska ordained Deacon Ishmael Gromoff of St. Paul Island as a priest to be assigned to the Unalaska parish. Chief Bill Dyakanoff sent a congratulatory telegram on behalf of the community. Once again a priest occupied the position which had been held by numerous illustrious predecessors: Veniaminov— St. Innocent of the Aleutians; Innokentii Shaishnikoff and Nikolai Rysev—Aleut priests and linguists; Alexander Kedrovsky—builder of the Holy Ascension Cathedral, community organizer, victim of a Soviet purge; Alexander Panteleev, future Bishop of Alaska; Father Basil Nagosky, later Metropolitan Vladimir, Bishop of Japan.

Father Ishmael came from a family with a flair for community service. His father was active in the attempts of the Pribilof people to secure their rights as American citizens. He, too, was later ordained a priest. Ishmael's sister Alexandra was an energetic champion of Aleut causes. It was natural that Father Gromoff would eventually involve himself in city and school councils. To supplement the small stipend he received from the local congregation, Father eventually became an Aleut language and craft instructor in the school. Prior to that he worked briefly in the post office and Phil would solemnly refer to "Our father who works in the post office." His wife, Platonida Gromoff, was a skilled health practitioner and soon became the village health aide. She, with Father, eventually became the mainstay of Aleut culture instruction in the public school.

Father Gromoff arrived at Unalaska and held his first service Saturday evening, May 3, 1966, with Andrew Makarin as Reader.

Those months, from the winter of 1965 to the spring of 1967, there were too many deaths. Clement Kochuten died on November 5. Alex Berikoff disappeared while hunting on December 23. Rufus Choate, with his wife Alice and children, had transferred their cattle ranch from Montana to Unalaska in 1963 and 1964, and on May 17, 1966, he died. Arthur and Elsie Lekanoff drowned in July. George Borenin died that summer and the valiant Augusta Galaktionoff succumbed to cancer on August 20. In September Philip Galaktionoff died two weeks after Helen Merculieff's sudden death. In November Anfesia noted in her diary the deaths of Sergie Artemenoff and Nellie Gould, her longtime friend at False Pass.

And which winter was it I lay in bed and thought I heard a voice? A brief weak distortion of the wind before I fell asleep? The next morning, however, one of Polly and Nick's children found a man's body in the snow. He was an older man who had come to Unalaska to work in a cannery and had died of an apparent heart attack while walking home through a storm.

Then on the afternoon of December 4, 1966, Alice Hope died in Washington state. The next day a service for this deeply loved woman was held at Unalaska, and when her body arrived five days later, Anfesia assisted Father Ishmael Gromoff in yet another service. Anfesia stayed all night with her departed friend, in the company of the Hope children and grandchildren and friends, until the service at the church on December 11. Anfesia noted in her diary, "had Liturgy with Mrs. Hope's body after funeral service walked her up all the way." Carrying the coffin the length of the village from the church to the graveyard was an act of uncommon devotion. More frequently the coffin was placed in a pickup and the mourners rode or walked behind.

Alice Hope's death came at the end of a long, productive life. Andrew's granddaughter's husband died at the beginning of his adulthood, shot by a family acquaintance who was drunk. Lance Craig was eighteen.

I had hiked to and back from Captain's Bay that afternoon, January 2, 1967, and in the evening I decided to walk out again, so beautiful was the winter night. Stars and moon illumined the snowy slopes from Mount Pyramid to the brown tangles of salmonberry bushes shredding the edge of the road. The ochre cliffs at Obernoi Point were dark, the weight of the island balanced against the sea.

While I chatted with Ruth and Gordon Craig and a visiting friend, their two younger sons horsed around the house finishing up a dessert Ruth had made. A few hundred yards away in their own home, Lance and Anna were playing cards with her father and Lance's sister while their infant daughter slept in the next room. Their game was interrupted by a knock at the door. Lance opened it. Shots from a revolver lit the night. The boy fell backward onto the floor.

His parents reached him before he died.

He became so white.

There was so little blood.

Anfesia was at the Center visiting Addie Nordstrom when I returned late that night. She stayed until eleven-thirty and went home as snow was beginning. The snowfall thickened all night, clogging the airport runway, blocking the road to Captain's Bay, delaying the arrival of the state trooper for days.

Lance's body was placed in a freezer building to preserve it for the required autopsy that would have to be done in Anchorage. I accompanied Andrew to visit Lance as he rested in that cold, vacuous building. The old man knew what he was doing.

On January 9 a funeral was held at the Bahá'í Center at 3 P.M. Eventually the body was returned and a graveside burial service was held on January 22, a day that rain and snow made brown and gray, white and black. We softened his grave's wound with fir branches cut from discarded Christmas trees.

The community had wrapped itself in sympathy around his and Anna's families, helping to construct and decorate a coffin, helping with the placement of the body, bringing food and comfort. Out of her unfathomable sorrow, Ruth found strength to deflect the anger so many felt toward her son's murderer, and to see him for what he was, to see her son's death for what it was. For his gravestone Ruth and Gordon selected a passage from Bahá'u'lláh's meditations *The Hidden Words*, which began, "O Son of Justice! Whither can a lover go but to the land of his beloved?"

Anfesia and Phil stayed at the Bahá'í Center the night of the funeral. Again on January 12, they were there late in the evening. I don't remember why they were there, but the presence of friends was always comforting. Because it was forty days after the death of Mrs. Hope, Anfesia and Phil excused themselves to go to her home for the memorial service. This was the same home where a few months before the friends of Helen Merculieff had gathered for a service the night of a tidal wave warning. Before long Anfesia and Phil returned, having found the house dark. Ruth Perez, Lance's grandmother, suggested the remembrance be observed at the Center, and so it was. Phil's melodious bass braided with his mother's fierce, keening soprano as they intoned portions of the service.

Lord, have mercy. Lord, have mercy. Lord, have mercy.

Christ, have mercy.

Ruth read that prayer by Bahá'u'lláh for the departed which contains the words, "Glorified art Thou, O my God! If Thou ceasest to be merciful unto Thy servants, who, then, will show mercy unto them? and if Thou refusest to succor Thy loved ones, who is there that can succor them?"

That year I learned I could not measure even my own belief. I had witnessed faith illumine acts in ways justice and knowledge could not. If I reached any certainty it was that faith was powerless and transcended courage. It could be neither maligned nor defended. It vanished whenever lines of differences were drawn and therefore had nothing to do with religion as we knew it. It cherished all doctrines.

When I learned that as a Bahá'í I should seek military registration as a noncombatant, I began the paperwork to have the draft board in my hometown change my classification. School ended in May, and I began courses at a college in Ellensburg, Washington, to complete the requirements for a degree in education. I had decided to become a teacher. Midway through the quarter, I received the conscientious objector status (1-A-O) and almost simultaneously I was drafted, sent to Fort Sam Houston, Texas, for several weeks of training, and by April 1968, I had arrived in Vietnam and been assigned to the 101st Airborne Division. A medic. A twenty-six-year-old goddamned medic.

Even though I was absent from Unalaska, people continued to flood me with kindness. From Helen Lekanoff came letters flush with scoldings, advice, and affection. Polly wrote to tell me about the deaths of her father Mike Kudrin and of Irene Galaktionoff. From Anfesia there came news, opinions, and a valiant attempt— somewhat fruitless, I'm afraid—to continue Aleut lessons through correspondence. She had earlier translated a Bahá'í prayer into Aleut for me and now she occasionally enclosed other translations in her letters. She kept me informed about Addie Nordstrom who was in failing health.

"Dear soul, when I see her I am happy," she wrote. Concerned about a friend's drinking, Anfesia found comfort in sitting with the older woman while Addie braided a rug from wool scraps and Anfesia knitted a pair of gloves.

"Whenever I give up on her I think of Addie's words that she is sick, say a prayer for her. Dear soul, I hope she feels better. She was so happy to see me. She held my hand so long."

Anfesia had always signed her letters "A. Shapsnikoff" or some variation of *uchiitilan ilan* (your teacher) but now she began closing her letters with *anaadan* (mother) or *Unangam ilan anaan* (your Aleut mom). For my part, I continued weaving with some raffia and a small bundle of prepared Unalaska basket grass.

I began a diary but soon learned this was against regulations and so started to weave specific designs into a small basket to remind me of events. Looking at the soiled grass weaving today, however, there is much I have forgotten. A running line of fifteen triangles outlined in green and colored gold, fuchsia, brown, black, and red at the top perhaps once represented the low hills outside Phuoc Vinh where I found permanent duty in the aid station of the 1/506th Infantry Battalion. I cannot remember why I wove a band of light green and blue diamonds—perhaps the fresh deceptive beauty of the Central Highlands? But those fourteen black dashes—those I remember inserting from wisps of black plastic I unraveled from sandbags at Dak To.

Then comes a complex design, part-geometry, part-bird, that I wove during a strange and solitary week back at Phuoc Vinh. Immediately on this are five somber rows of solid brown and blackened gray recalling dreadful weeks at Cu Chi when casualties multiplied like fungus, and we lost so many men. Then a row of brilliant red squares interrupted by a streak of blue: sweet Phuoc Vinh; beautiful Phuoc Vinh; Phuoc Vinh, U.S.A. After this the basket is torn, the warp cut close.

When the battalion moved north and established a base camp near Hue, I started again—weaving a round base and coming up the sides. A gray, desolate border interspersed with brightly colored dots was woven among some ancient tombs where we erected our tents, and recalls nights I spent with two friends from Reconn, Jim Lewis and Edward Scott III. The weaving terminates with a barrage of green and blue arrows rushing towards nothingness. I wove these while the unit began preparations for an offensive, which occurred a couple of weeks after I returned to the States and which became notorious for the attack on Hamburger Hill.

On December 1, 1967, Anfesia wrote me a letter. Vince, the grandson she had raised, was now in the Navy. Another grandson was in the Marines. I was in the Army. Soon we would all be in Vietnam. She wrote:

> Long time ago in my early days when I had tea parties with salt
> fish and dry Aleut bread, I use to hear them sit and talk over their tea

*cup, saying, "Yes! They will start things we never hear or see, objects will appear in sky and human people will start against one another. At that time things will get harder for boy child. Those days we hope not to see." Then I would wonder what they mean by that. Now I live to see it all, so I must have lived half century.*

Having studied the generation to which those old persons sitting at tea belonged, I cannot imagine how circumstances could have become harsher than what they themselves had experienced. For them a culture had neared extinction.

In November 1967, I had written to Anfesia from basic training asking if Jimmy Krukoff, a boy of six or seven, could become my *atcha*. Anfesia had earlier arranged for Father Ishmael Gromoff and me to be *atchas* after she discovered that my birthday and the day of his ordination were the same. An *atcha* is something like a partner, something like a brother or sister, something like an alternate self. Once when Anfesia began scolding me fiercely, I was completely bewildered until I realized she was criticizing my *atcha* through me. In her letters she often referred to Father Gromoff as "your silent *atcha*."

Jimmy was one of many children in a remarkable family that exhibited a strength and cohesion that dumbfounded the village. Anfesia's reply was not what I had expected.

On November 13, she wrote that Bill Dyakanoff, chief of Unalaska, "our Chief and friend," had died. Doc's generosity resulted in his having a host of *atchas*, and Jimmy had been one of them. Jimmy had shared Doc's name and so when Anfesia approved our being *atchas*, she wrote, "Now when you come back we have to call you *Qumatu*, meaning getting white." Then she added, "We won't have trouble calling you that." A year later she wrote, "Did I tell you what *Qumatu* means (lots of white) so old Doc never let them tell him he was old."

When I arrived at the infantry battalion, the first sergeant had said conscientious objectors were not permitted in the field. The battalion surgeon refused to release me to Headquarters Company as a clerk, and I remained thankfully at the aid station. Near the close of my tour, the unit received several new medics who were conscientious objectors, and they all went to line companies. By then, however, I was neither surprised nor offended by the innocent duplicity of military administration. Apart from occasional medcaps, where medicines and simple treatments were given to people in nearby villages, and eventually a stint assisting English lessons to Catholic sisters at an orphanage, I was rarely outside the perimeter of our various base camps.

I organized daily sick calls, wrote reports, and occasionally represented the doc at battalion meetings. As the magical 365th day of my tour neared, I was encouraged to extend with the promise of another promotion and an "early out." I refused. I was promoted to staff sergeant. I "rotated" to the States. A letter from Unalaska inviting me back to teach freed me a few weeks early from the supervision of an aid station at Fort Leonard Wood, Missouri.

I returned to Unalaska. Andrew Makarin had died. Addie Nordstrom had died. Doc's position as chief was not filled. Swollen with money from the king crab boom, the town had reorganized itself and began emerging as one of the major fishing ports in the United States. With more non-Native families in town, the school board extended education beyond the eighth grade. A few high school teachers were hired, and their work was supplemented by correspondence courses.

I was asked to organize a non-graded primary program, a philosophy temporarily espoused by the State Department of Education. Military service had interrupted my pursuit of a teacher's certification, and so I was again hired under emergency provisions, the last choice, when no one else was available.

I had chameleons and gerbils in the classroom. The lizards survived on flies cooled into immobility in the school attic. The gerbils produced a frantic call from Nellie Bereskin one afternoon. She had been cleaning my room and saw a rag floating in the sink. The drain was frequently clogged and when the water dripped it filled the basin. When she reached for the rag, it quivered. The gerbils had turned into lemmings and drowned themselves in the sink.

When I didn't have time or inclination for the trek to Agamgik or Ugadaga, I sometimes climbed the long road on the northeast side of

Unalaska Valley into the Ski Bowl. Dozens of Quonsets, cabanas, and barracks spread across the high valley where the military had built a small ski tow below the final steep ascent to the summit. The longest building standing was a theater/library. The theater floor had collapsed under the weight of stacked wooden benches. The library half of the building had shelves and no books. Nevertheless, it was the only library in town, and I sometimes carried a book there and would sit in an open window frame on a calm day and read.

Eventually Marianna Foliart began a school library. The principal, Fred Kent, had partitioned a small room off the gym and Marianna made an heroic attempt to stock the room with books. When Senator Ernest Gruening and his entourage visited Unalaska they were given a tour of the school. This former newspaperman, governor of the territory during the war, early governor of the new state, author of a major history of Alaska and of numerous scholarly articles, paused before the bleak wall of books while his companions pressed into the gym. He was silent as he scanned the shelves, pulled out a volume, read its title page, and replaced it with a slight shake of his head. For me his silence was an eminent critique of educational opportunities in rural Alaska.

At least the Ski Bowl library had a view.

## ANDREW MAKARIN VISITS
## THE BODY OF LANCE CRAIG

After and because we had
suspended the disintegration of violence
by freezing his body
when the storm blew for days,
(finally a plane, a marshal, interrogations,
his thawed wounds bleeding for science)
the old man asked to see him.
I don't remember what I thought
as we pulled the weighted door of the cold storage building.

Outside the ice-scaled lake's reptilian stillness
held a cold we could not equal.
I expected him to speak Aleut or recite
something liturgical in Russian. Those were his languages.
But he bent down carefully
the high language of his ancestors laid aside.
I remember
the courtesy, the clarity, the deference to the dead,
that although fluency was lacking there should be no mistake.
He said, "Hello, dead boy."

I had seen Andrew
huddled in the fold of a hill,
before the river had washed the lake of ice
and the last gust of winter shook the house.
Until startled, both invisible.
He was looking across the lake,
over ice and rock, beyond the pass, down to Ugadaga Bay
where his skiff was shelved on a high bank, anchored forever,
the tides of storming grass engulfing it.
His village beyond the bay was abandoned.
The history of his family had ended.
There was not even a quiet complaint.

Somewhere baidarka models rest
labeled with numbers, nameless. But those by Andrew
dream of water. On these treeless islands
I will tell you a secret.
A man burned yellow cedar.
He burned the sea's gift.
For the scent of yellow cedar,
because the scent of yellow cedar
pleased the one he loved,
a man burned what enabled him to survive.

# 10

# Turning Corners

Comparing a recent school administrator with a former one, the storekeeper leaned toward me and took me into his confidence, "At least he kept his prick in his pocket."

*Christ,* I thought, *what kind of a profession am I in?*

The village was shoulder-deep in late March snowdrifts. School had been canceled. The snowplow had succumbed to water in its fuel line, and people stood with shovels near their doors weighing the probability of a melting rain. The store opened late, but was open when I got there. I bought a sack of cookies and two magazines.

Verne smiled, "Something to keep you warm?"

I laughed, embarrassed. *True Adventures* with its bosomy cover announced that "A Lion Ate My Wife" and that Hitler's secret hoard of gold had been discovered in South America. I'd heard about this issue and definitely wanted a copy. I opened to the article on Hitler and showed Verne where a photo caption read, "There was much singing and dancing in the village. After that came a wild orgy. In the morning, we all went off to search for the treasure buried in the mountains." Covering a page and a half of the article was a photograph of Unalaska before the war. Another photo showed late nineteenth-century Aleut dwellings with salmon drying on racks. Verne started coughing, broke into laughter, and gave me an example of language as subtle as the photographs in many of the magazines he stocked. Then changing the subject to the school, he leaned toward me and took me into his confidence.

Of course, I bought the other magazine for its interview.

I was beginning to learn something about Unalaska's past—usually from sources more reliable than *True Adventures*. Because the Chain and other coastal areas of Alaska had been explored and settled before the Interior, Hubert Howe Bancroft's 1886 *History of Alaska* was filled with choice Aleutian nuggets. Bancroft had sent Ivan Petroff to gather information in the territory, and he had traveled throughout the Chain in the 1870s. He later wrote his own extensive geographical and historical summaries for various editions of the 1880 Census. Veins of extraordinary interest ran through his work. I hoarded it all, ignorant that before long historical assessors (Richard Pierce, Lydia Black, Morgan Sherwood, Theodore Hinckley, and Michael Oleksa) would prove Petroff's claims false, his choice nuggets rarely anything but pyrite.

Aleutian history as recounted by Anfesia involved stories of particular people interacting with the land, with traditions, and with each other.

For me history was simply a record of changes. I think for Anfesia, however, and here I am probably being presumptuous, history was an anecdotal record illuminating the continuity of a people. History was driven by the characteristics of the people who were the subject of the history. History could end.

She told me once how old-time Aleuts used to say that February and March quarreled with each other. February would say that although it had only twenty-eight days and was short, it could still make worse weather than March. March disputed this. Old men sitting around during a storm would say, "It's March quarreling with February."

She told me about the blind storyteller Cedor [Isidor] Solovyov who lived from 1849 to 1912. Shortly after he moved to Unalaska from Akutan, an earthquake caused the tip of the peninsula to sink into the bay. Perhaps he willingly tempted fate, but in any event his *barabara*, the traditional semi-subterranean home so suited to Aleutian weather, was located near the dock.

Anfesia remembered seeing him walk the length of the shore to the Jesse Lee Home orphanage and boarding school, where he would sing and tell stories for the children. In 1909 and 1910, a number of his stories were recorded by the Russian ethnologist Waldemar Jochelson. Many of these tales dealt with tragic accounts of love, jealousy, and war and ended with the deaths of the protagonists.

It was ironic, then, that years after Cedor died, Thomas Snow arrived from the States and fell in love with an Aleut woman in Kashega. After a courtship he brought her to Unalaska, where they lived together. Unfortunately he had ignored the chief of Kashega and this man arrived, consulted with the chief of Unalaska, and took the woman back to her home village. Snow killed himself in the old *barabara* where blind Cedor had lived. After this suicide the *barabara* was torn down.

Anfesia had immense respect for the Unalaska chief Alexei Yatchmenef, who lived from 1866 to 1937. All accounts left by visitors to Unalaska recall him as a man of great dignity, warmth, and learning. He became chief around 1900 and remained in that position until his death. One afternoon Anfesia said, "Alexei was chief for all those years, and never lost his temper. Just one time," she added with emphasis, "did I ever see him raise his voice. I never forgot."

She warned me that it was a long story, but I had lots of time.

The priest at Unalaska in those days was a young Russian immigrant. Energetic and ambitious, he would become a prominent figure in the Chain in the years when fox trapping meant good money. Chief Alexei Yatchmenef had a large family and his second son was Peter. The priest's wife developed a love for Peter, but the young man did his best to ignore her. Nevertheless, she continued seeking him out, especially when her husband was off on his pastoral duties to other villages.

Upon his return from one trip, the priest visited Anfesia and her husband, Michael Tutiakoff, and asked if they knew what his wife had been doing. They knew, of course, but they wouldn't say anything. "We don't know anything about what she does," they said.

Sophie Pletnikoff's sister, Aleta, was helping to care for the priest's two young children in their home. At this time Anfesia was carrying her first child and spent much of her time visiting old man Peter Krukoff, who lived close to the priest's home. Her daughter Martha would be born in May 1920.

One night Peter Yatchmenef and some other men were playing cards, probably at the Iliuliuk Club. The priest's wife was there also and a man named Byers slipped a note under the priest's door informing him of this.

Later the priest always said you could never kill a person unless his time was up. No matter how hard you tried you couldn't do it if the time for that person's death had not arrived. Because of this you should not condemn yourself for what you do.

The priest was livid and took his rifle and loaded it with three shells: one for Peter, one for his wife, and one for himself. He sent word for Peter to come to his house. Aleta was taking care of the two children. When she heard Peter at the door she took the children upstairs but stayed on the steps and saw what happened. The priest accused Peter of attempting to seduce his wife. Peter replied that he didn't know what this was about. The priest should ask his wife, not him, about what was going on because he wasn't after his wife. Maybe she was after him, but he didn't know.

In a rage, the priest struck the young man in the jaw and knocked him through the door, breaking one of the panels. Peter fell to the ground and as he pulled himself up he told himself that this was an ordained priest and he must not hit an ordained priest. He just stood with his hands to his side and the priest became even more enraged at Peter's refusal to fight. He took his rifle and pulled the trigger but nothing happened. He cocked it and again it refused to fire. Grabbing the rifle by the barrel the priest struck him on the side of the head and Peter fell unconscious to the floor. The priest ran from the house as Aleta came down the stairs. She couldn't leave the two small children, but Peter was almost dead, and she thought the priest was heading to the dock to throw himself in the bay.

The priest, however, returned with Byers, who swung Peter over his shoulder and carried him to his father's home. Anfesia saw Peter carried through the churchyard. He was unconscious as they approached the church but upon entering the yard, Peter came to but he was still very groggy. As they left the churchyard, he again lapsed into unconsciousness.

Alexei Yatchmenef would not allow the priest into his house, so deep was his anger. Blocking the door, the chief shouted and cried at the priest for what he had done. Anfesia overheard this and was very moved. Innokenti Petikoff, a man skilled in traditional healing, stayed with Peter for three days until he regained consciousness. The side of his head was always somewhat flat.

This took place in the fall. There was low fog all around. The priest remained through the winter and in the spring moved away. That fall, however, the priest put his wife on a ship leaving Unalaska. He wanted no more trouble. As it happened the vessel was carrying men off to trap on different islands and unknown to the priest among the men was Peter Yatchmenef. For years the men at Unalaska—Peter, Michael Tutiakoff, Peter Dushkin's father, and others—would laugh over Peter's trip with the priest's wife. The priest had said he would live to bury both Peter and his wife, but, Anfesia said, even now Peter and the priest's wife are still alive and he has been dead a long time.

"I tell Peter," Anfesia laughed, "'That priest is dead now. Why don't you marry his wife?' He laughs and says, 'She never meant anything to me.'"

There are at least three valuable insights into Aleut life in the early twentieth century in this story about Alexei Yatchmenef. The first is Anfesia's account of how Peter regained consciousness upon entering the churchyard but lost it when he was carried outside its perimeter. The sacredness of the church was not destroyed or weakened by the violent action of the priest. Indeed, the church itself seemed to affirm Peter's innocence. The second point is shown in Aleta's refusal to leave the children in order to get aid for Peter or to prevent the priest from harming himself. This is a clear statement of priorities in Aleut society and is confirmed by other accounts. Finally, the chief's refusal to admit the priest into his house was an act of almost unparalleled defiance. For all practical purposes, the priest's position in Aleut society was above that of the chief; the priest was given preference over the chief or any other leader. Peter's refusal to defend himself against the priest suggests a status difference of quality.

Alexei Yatchmenef's devotion to his church never wavered. Already by 1898 the bishop had recognized him for his work in the construction of the new church at Unalaska. This devotion remained to the end.

Anfesia told me that only when Alexei was dying did he relinquish the church keys. He sent them to William Zaharoff to assure a smooth transition from one leader to another.

With magazines and cookies tucked into my knapsack, I followed the path through the snow back toward home until I saw footprints leading in the direction of Anfesia's house. The tracks continued past her yard and on to Hilda Berikoff's place. I brushed snow off my pants and boots while her son Phil wrestled to unlock the door.

"*Aang*, Qumatu," Anfesia said. "You're up early."

Phil had boiled a pot of coffee, stilling and sinking the grounds with a dash of cold water. He poured hot water into a cup, emptied it, filled it with coffee and handed it to me. I sat in the deep comfortable chair placed in the corner under the family icons. Anfesia was on the couch, an afghan she had crocheted wrapped around her, thumbing through a book she had borrowed from Father Gromoff, Aleš Hrdlička's mammoth volume on Aleut prehistory with its catalog of excerpts from accounts written by eighteenth- and nineteenth-century explorers.

From Dall's random digging in the 1870s to Jochelson's systematic excavations in 1909 and 1910, from Weyer's brief visit in 1929 to Hrdlička's sweeps through the islands in 1936, 1937, and 1938, the infrequent archaeological work in the Aleutians provided little information about contemporary life. Historians concentrated on events outside the Chain.

The arrival of Russians in the Aleutians and the development of the Russian American Company (most of which occurred at Kodiak and Sitka) were topics generally covered in histories of Alaska. After the purchase of Alaska in 1867, except for the international brouhaha over fur seals at the turn of the century, the Aleutians vanished from histories, receding into their proverbial fog until Japanese planes broke through in 1942. Published accounts by travelers occasionally mentioned the islands. Although anthropologists were better trained than tourists to evaluate or comment on local events, their interest lay in whatever might suggest the life that existed among Aleut people prior to or at the time of first contact with the West.

Nevertheless, anthropologists served another purpose. In a region where research was as rare as it was expensive and arduous, the Aleutian Islands saw anthropologists supply villagers with role models of hostility. The networks of relationships among villages in the Chain kept local folks apprised of the comings and goings, the skirmishes and retreats, the eccentricities and jealousies of visiting bonediggers. Their feuds and infidelities sweetened many winter conversations over tea long after the scientists had returned to their universities to write up the summer's discoveries.

Anfesia had little use for published information on Aleuts.

"I see my granddad's name there," she said as she closed the book, "but he was not from Amchitka. Damn people, lies and lies. Never say anything true about Aleuts."

Sought out by visiting scholars, she usually welcomed them, answered their questions, and occasionally took them with her to fish camp. In return she hoped they would send her copies of the articles they wrote, but somehow they usually forgot to do this. What was sent was, in her view, too often skewed, too frequently filled with supposition and error. The past summer she had written to me about the two weeks anthropologists had spent at her fish camp.

"Not one can of food did they bring," she wrote, still angry at having had to feed them while she answered their endless questions. "Who else could do that for nothing—that's what *promyshlenniks* do, intruders, whites do."

*Promyshlenniks* were the Russian fur hunters stereotyped in popular fiction as blood-thirsty invaders who pillaged Aleut communities and slaughtered thousands. The reality of the historical record is less dramatic and far more complicated. Anfesia's reference to these hunters reflected her stay in Kodiak during the summers of 1968 and 1969, when she again taught Aleut basketry classes for the Kodiak Historical Society. While there she was talked into playing a small role in *The Cry of the Wild Ram*, a local play about Alexander Baranov, the early Russians, and the discovery of Kodiak Island with its fierce Native population.

"I'm the Aleut they found," she joked. While on stage she had to squat down and weave a basket. However, as a nineteenth-century Aleut she couldn't wear her glasses, and consequently she couldn't see what she was doing. She thought of having Unalaska put on its own pageant and suggested I would play "one of the mean Russian teachers with a violin."

The *promyshlenniks* of the play provided a term to describe people she'd witnessed in the Chain throughout her life, people who came to the islands only for what they could take away, people with little concern for local Aleuts. Writing about the mayor she said, "Old — don't have mercy for no one at all. . . . These people may mean well but I think they are taking advantage of the Natives. They don't try to help them but to hurt them." And on another town official, "He came here and got what he wanted, and now he turns us down. If it wasn't for Aleuts he wouldn't have a job. Because he is the head he thinks he has to take over and get things all his own way. Well, he resigned and now he wants his job back. No way. We can always find one that will stick with the Aleuts and not look down on us. . . . But I have to tell him I have seen dirty whites, too, and drunk ones, too."

And then she added, "OK, OK. I am alone and I have no one else to put up with or tell, so I had to write it."

I took my empty cup out to the kitchen, refilled it, and returned to sit next to Anfesia. Frail and brittle but remarkably resolute, she could eat only small amounts of food at one time. Phil was stretched out on a blanket in front of the stove putting the final touches to a carved letter opener. The curves on its handle were like folded waves.

Phil's wood carvings were at once evocative of the Aleutian landscape and of the curved designs on eighteenth- and nineteenth-century Aleut wooden hats. These masterpieces of early Aleut art were made from select driftwood that was carved, steamed, bent, and tied into an elongated cone whose front sloped like a long visor. Elaborated with ivory carvings, beads, and smoky wisps of sea lion whiskers, the whole hat was painted with lavish bands. Occasionally these bands broke into curves like mirrored leaves or crested waves. Below the peak, a spectacular open spiral dominated each side. Phil rarely carved anything larger than what he could hold in the palm of his hand: letter openers and lidded snuff boxes, a comb to grace a woman's hair, a rattle for the child of a friend. Yellow cedar was a favorite wood along with scrub alder that had washed ashore: The salt water intensified the colors in the grain.

Anfesia saw her youngest son as the hope of many family dreams, but Philemon Tutiakoff had his own dreams, his own demons. His mind was too critical to accommodate compromises without gut-wrenching consequences to himself; yet he often found himself in positions where compromises were essential—serving on boards for health and social services, on local and regional Aleut boards, working as a director for non-profit Native corporations and getting paid, as he said, less than Jesus. He held odd jobs—in the post office, as health aide, as a part-time social worker. He made a few runs at completing a college degree.

Thunder is rare in the Aleutians. Phil remarked once that when he was a child and heard thunder for the first time an old man told him it was the sound of *baidars*—large open flat-bottomed skin boats—pulled up the beach over driftwood logs in the sky. Phil was as rare as thunder: An articulate mind refracted through the facets of a culture at once traditional and compellingly new. However aggravating his work with committees and individuals became at times, he always referred to Aleuts as "the best people on earth." Through his mother he became my "brot," my brother.

As I sat down beside Anfesia, I showed her a copy of an old letter

I had received from the University of Alaska Archives in Fairbanks. Clara Goodwin Goss had taught school at Unalaska around the turn of the century. She had been one of Henry Swanson's teachers. I told Anfesia I'd leave the long letter with her, but I read out loud where Clara and her husband, A.C. Goss, on November 16, 1913, had accompanied the new chief of Atka into the attic of the church where they found eight old icons. Clara Goss was an avid collector of Aleut baskets, Russian samovars, and icons. She and her husband had paid the chief five dollars for the old icons. Anfesia's eyes darkened.

"Mrs. Goss's house burned up and all her baskets, all her icons. She couldn't even save a sock from among her belongings." The fire occurred in the winter, in the time around the two Christmases. The community was having a masquerade party upstairs in the A.C. Company hall. Everyone was dressed in heavy costumes. Mr. Goss was on a trip out west on his vessel. Mrs. Goss was visiting at one of the missionary houses on the east end of town. The Goss home was midway between the mission and the A.C. Company. People at the party looked out a window and saw fire engulf the building. Nothing was saved.

"Mrs. Snigeroff told me this later," Anfesia continued. An old woman from Atka, a relative of hers, had put those icons in the church for safekeeping. When she learned of the secret sale, she wept a great deal. No one had a right to sell them, the old woman said. They belonged to the church. God would not allow anyone to use them.

History is such an accident of record. Anfesia told me a few stories about her life. I stumbled upon a few others. She attended the government school where she learned English. One afternoon, as she sat behind Edith Newhall, the fair-haired daughter of beloved missionaries, she couldn't resist dipping a blond pigtail into the inkwell. Noah and Clara Davenport, her teachers from 1910 to 1912, hired her to help around their home after the birth of their first child. She went to class at the Russian School after the day at the government school was over. Here she learned to read and write Aleut and Russian. Once when she failed to do an assignment, she was disciplined by having to kneel for several hours on the hard wooden floor of the church.

Chief Alexei Yatchmenef had arranged both of Anfesia's marriages, both in the aftermath of great loss. In 1918 or 1919 her mother, working through the chief, was sounding out the possibility of her daughter marrying Philip Tutiakoff's son Michael. He was seven years older than Anfesia and even though he was somewhat crippled (enough to prevent him becoming an active hunter) he seemed to have a promising future. Anfesia's father and Michael's mother had died some years before. Before the marriage plans were settled the 1919 flu epidemic struck Unalaska, and both Anfesia's mother and Michael's father died. Alexei Yatchmenef concluded the arrangements for their marriage. Through the 1920s, Michael Tutiakoff was able to support a growing family while gaining a position of leadership in the Aleut community.

I literally dug up a document that illustrated the spunk with which Anfesia pursued her goals. One day as I hiked through the dump on my way to Summer Bay I noticed a lot of old yellow paper sticking up through the dirt and grass. Investigating I found pages of correspondence written in the early 1930s by the manager of the Alaska Commercial Company store. I saved what was salvageable. Among the letters was one dated November 3, 1932. In it the manager wrote that Anfesia ("Mrs. Mike Tutiakoff") and a delegation of women from the Orthodox Sisterhood had asked to use the A.C. Company's hall for a masked dance on October 31. A Coast Guard vessel was expected in and the Sisterhood planned to charge ten cents for admission to raise money for "their charities in the village." The agent would not allow them to charge admission, as this was against a company policy. Instead he donated ten dollars to compensate for the loss of door receipts.

The town's movie theater, The Blue Fox Theater, was operated by a white couple. They, too, had planned a Halloween dance but now decided to show a ten-reel film to try to lure some of the visiting sailors. When Anfesia and some Sisterhood women called on the theater owners and requested the movie not be shown, they "were refused with some heat." The agent wrote, "Quite a number of sailors were at the theater door waiting to get in when the ladies said, 'Come on, boys, we are going to start the dance now.' I am told more than half the men followed along to the dance hall." The dance was attended by Aleuts, the crew and officers of the *Northland*, and all the white people except the owners of the theater. When it became known the dance was a charity affair, the men made voluntary contributions.

By 1932 Michael had been made a Deacon in the church, and there was the possibility of priestly ordination before him. There were young children in the family: Martha, Vincent, Tracy, Timothy, and Philemon. Another girl, Mayme, had died in infancy. In July 1932, Michael traveled with Bishop Antonin to Attu, and the following January he accompanied him on a trip west aboard the *Umnak Native*, a vessel owned by the Native community of Nikolski. A prolonged violent storm cornered the vessel in Inanudak Bay on Umnak Island. Prior to the sale of the *Umnak Native* to Nikolski village, its original engine had been replaced by an inferior one. Now the engine failed and the vessel broke apart. Eleven people, including Anfesia's husband, died from drowning or exposure. The bishop and a few others survived.

A lamp rested on a square wooden table next to my chair, and below the lamp was a framed photograph of Michael Tutiakoff holding his youngest son, Phil.

Anfesia was alone with children to clothe and feed. During the next few years their life became burdensome. The church and her relatives helped, but she faced the realization that the authorities might take her children from her. She had alienated several of the white residents who were in positions of influence. Once again, Alexei Yatchmenef, now a very old man, arranged a marriage for her. Just eight months before the chief's own death, she married the widower Sergie Shapsnikoff in February 1937. Although Sergie's family was from Unalaska (his grandfather Michael had been born there) his father, Elia, had served as chief of Makushin village for about ten years. Sergie was a good provider. He and Anfesia formally adopted two children, Kathryn and Gregory. Reflecting the fondness with which he was held, Sergie Shapsnikoff was called "Friend" by all the children.

When Anfesia was a young girl, a priest named Alexander Panteleev served Unalaska. In the late 1930s, he returned as Bishop Alexei for an extended stay in the Aleutians. While at Unalaska he blessed Anfesia as a Reader in the church. With the security of a stable household, Anfesia once again became a point of reference for the town, not only as a Reader during church services, but as someone able to communicate with various officials. Much of her energy was centered on training her eldest son, Vincent, to follow in the footsteps of his father. By 1942 he had served as Acting Warden for the church and as President and Secretary of the church committee.

After the death of Chief Alexei Yatchmenef, the new Chief and Primary Warden of the Church, William Zaharoff, was overwhelmed by the arrival of what must have seemed like most of the residents of the United States landing on his small island. He had neither the skills nor inclination to negotiate with the military and commercial barrage that constructed the base on Amaknak Island. Immense money swept into the village.

The U.S. Commissioner, certainly one of Anfesia's *promyshlenniks*, whom Henry Swanson called "a crook, but an honest crook," cornered as much rentable real estate as possible. He led the drive to incorporate the village as a first-class city in order to have better leverage in dealing with the government. He got the chief to be the first signer on the petition requesting incorporation—a petition signed by nearly as many transient workers as residents, a petition not signed by Anfesia. He opened a whorehouse on a small island in the channel between Unalaska and Amaknak Islands. The skiff ride to the island was inexpensive, but the trip away from Pecker Point cost ten times the initial fare. Eventually the establishment closed and the military filled in the narrow channel separating Expedition Island from Amaknak.

"We're going over to Peter and Laresa's at noon," Phil said. "Why don't you join us?"

"Peter coming over in his skiff?" I asked. The Dushkins lived on

Amaknak Island, where Peter worked for one of the crab canneries.

"We'll be back by five or so," Anfesia said. "Church tonight."

"Sure," I said. "Thanks."

Anfesia had reopened Hrdlička to a 1932 photograph of the residents of Attu village. The photographer must have been standing on top of a building. As I sat beside her, she named the people beginning with the late chief Mike Hodikoff. She identified all sixteen adults including Jenny Krukoff and the legendary weaver Maggie Prokopeuff.

"I'll have to bring my Xerox copy over and write down those names," I said. She turned the page. There was Jenny Krukoff, her husband and family next to a photograph of Simeon Pletnikoff's parents. Anfesia pointed at Simeon's mother and said, "She was from St. Paul Island." I again marveled how she seemed to know every Aleut in the Aleutians.

The photograph on the next page showed three views of a severed head lifted from one of the Kagamil Island mummies. After a moment's pause, Anfesia said, "He doesn't look familiar."

We left her house by the front door and followed foot tracks out to the main road, where tire ruts had pressed a narrow path. Polly Lekanoff waved as she made her way down to Verne's store. Anfesia took the lead as we passed the partially shoveled approach to Henry Swanson's cabin. A snow shovel leaned against the house while Henry scratched behind the ears of a large woolly dog, one of several dogs that periodically used his house as a hotel. Ahead of us Sophie Pletnikoff turned into her daughter's house, and two Filipino cannery workers banged on the locked door of the post office.

"Must be sorting mail," Phil said. The new postmaster, Sophie Sherebernikoff, always locked the door when she sorted mail so as not to be disturbed. When he was abreast the impatient workers, Phil cupped his hands around his mouth and shouted, "It's a national holiday!"

Anfesia turned a startled face and said, "Doggone kid!"

Nick Lekanoff was shoveling a path from the road through the churchyard. Soon he would light the small oil stove in the Sergie Chapel for evening services.

When the military buildup began, the priest at Unalaska was Father Dionecious. By November 1941 the military had imposed certain rules regarding curfew, blackouts, and travel outside the immediate village. Sergie Shapsnikoff and another man, Sergie Shaishnikoff, were out west on one of the islands trapping fox.

Sergie Shaishnikoff's wife was ill with tuberculosis, and Anfesia had moved into her home to care for her. One night Vincent Tutiakoff and Chester Bereskin were across the town creek, near the reservoir at the base of Haystack. They noticed lights on in the church steeple, even though a blackout had been imposed. Vincent crossed the creek, found the church unlocked and went in. Father Dionecious was standing in the center of the main chapel directly beneath the great chandelier. Vincent spoke to him, but the priest just stood, staring, with his arms crossed over his chest, as though in a trance. Bewildered, Vincent walked up to him and finally Father Dionecious recognized him and said, "Someone has turned on the lights."

Vincent turned the lights off and walked the priest home. The next day military personnel came around asking Anfesia questions as only she and the priest were allowed keys to the church. She said after that she didn't trust the priest. He had served in Asia and she just didn't trust him.

Peter Dushkin was at the creek with his skiff when we clambered down the snowbank. Once we were seated he lashed the outboard into a controlled frenzy and took the curved channel out the mouth of the creek. Crossing the narrow trough of water to Amaknak, we passed Expedition Island and tied the skiff at a wooden dock where several other small boats were at rest. Peter and Laresa's trailer was one of four with a view back toward town. Laresa had hot soup and sandwiches waiting for us.

After lunch Peter, Laresa, Phil, and I played pinochle while

Anfesia curled her feet under her on a comfortable chair and knitted on a pair of navy-blue gloves. A CB radio hummed from its perch on top of the refrigerator while the two young Dushkin boys careened around the room. Whatever their drawbacks, the crab canneries had provided regular incomes for several Aleut families.

The arrival of the king crab industry at Unalaska had parallels with the construction boom that accompanied World War II. Both were directed by firms or agencies with headquarters elsewhere, who would have preferred to not have had a local population to contend with. Both involved the sudden arrival of large numbers of people anxious for quick money. Both resulted in a changed landscape.

Phil and Laresa had won the last hand. While I shuffled the cards, Laresa remarked, "I went looking for sea eggs with Mo, but, boy, the water was dirty."

Anfesia kept knitting and said, "The war broke up all our fishing grounds and our berry patches. There's just only the ruins of that left." And now, she continued, the crab and shrimp canneries have left the bays and beaches filthy. "We are unable to go out and pick any food off the beach which we lived on. And there is no fish in the bay because there is oil all over. The clams and mussels and things like that we went and ate, they are all dying from oil."

"Dang canneries!" Laresa laughed, acknowledging the irony.

Anfesia consistently maintained that the military and commercial presence in the Aleutians had polluted the sea and destroyed traditional fishing grounds. In the past streams had been clean, the water drinkable. Sea urchins could be harvested from the shores without fear of oil contamination. Because of the events of this century, Aleuts could no longer subsist from the earth: "Now if they left us like before we would starve because of all that." But Aleuts in the past had always survived, no matter how difficult the times. Now "we can, too, if we know how."

However, an even greater danger appeared.

"The only thing we went and had was the land," she said. "And now they don't want us to have the land. They're claiming most of our lands that we lived on."

The General Services Administration had decided the government should divest itself of the land it had claimed during World War II. Amaknak Island had been put on sale and the first parcels were sold. As a member of the city council Anfesia had served on the Board of Equalization, and she feared foreclosure when Aleuts who had little cash income were forced to pay taxes on land.

"Long time ago, very long time ago," she said, "I used to hear the old chief say this, that some of these days we'd be unable to have a land to live on. I didn't think I would live to see it and hear it and here I am."

In 1970 Walter Dyakanoff, William Berikoff, Henry Swanson, Nick Peterson, and Anfesia provided testimony on traditional subsistence use on Amaknak Island and other areas surrounding Unalaska. Represented by Alaska Legal Services Corporation, an arm of the federal Office of Economic Opportunity, Henry, Nick, and Anfesia were named in a civil lawsuit filed in January 1971 in the U.S. District Court in Anchorage. The suit asked that a restraining order be issued postponing the January 20 sale of land on Amaknak and Unalaska Islands. On January 17, a U.S. District judge halted the sale. In December 1971, President Richard Nixon signed the Alaska Native Claims Settlement Act, and a vast restructuring of power began in the state. One of the most pronounced impacts of the act on a local level was the transfer of the land that had been for sale on Amaknak and Unalaska to Aleut people.

Under the act, regional and local Native corporations were formed. The Aleut Corporation and the Ounalashka Corporation, regional and local bodies, began to enroll their members, to organize themselves, to formulate goals, and to define relationships with commercial, municipal, and state institutions. Aleuts who had been active on the city council or other community bodies found they had only so much time to give to service on boards and began concentrating on those that were most important: those that directly affected Aleut land and lifestyles.

We were back on the "Unalaska side" by four in the afternoon. The road had been plowed. We walked past the church and said hello to a woman who was shoveling snow from the low front steps at Doc's house. Edna Pelagia McCurdy was a cousin of the late chief, and she had been given permission to move into his house. In 1909, the year of her birth, the wife of a white fur trader had tried persuading Pelagia's mother to put her up for adoption and had written to the Child Rescue Department of New York City, "Little Pelagia is strong, active, and bright for her age. She has dark eyes, brown hair and a fair complexion. Her features are good and she has a most engaging smile."

Pelagia escaped adoption and spent much of her childhood at her grandparents' home on Hog Island, a small island within Unalaska Bay. Those same arresting eyes now lit by a critical intelligence were evident when she returned to Unalaska in 1967 after a full life in California, where she had retired from teaching. She came home hoping to help her people. Anfesia was overjoyed at her arrival and wrote to me that Pelagia was "pleasant and understanding, not like me."

Pelagia worked in the school as a librarian and tutor until she undertook the vast job of locating the descendents of Aleuts from Unalaska Island in order to enroll them under the Alaska Native Claims Settlement Act. She worked with Emil Berikoff, one of the first officers of the nascent Native organization at Unalaska. The job of enrollment was monumental. Years of oppression had encouraged some people to blend into the general blandness of American life, to divest themselves of being Aleut when being so meant being viewed with disdain or outright discrimination.

Anfesia lamented the fact that when a close friend visited family in the Lower 48 and became ill, the children who could not afford to take her to a general hospital would not take her to the Indian Health Service facilities because they did not want to be known as Aleuts. These were tragic situations for a people, but the formation of local and regional corporations gave a reason for reidentifying with ancestral ties. If the reasons were merely money and land and power, or the possibility of any of these, the reasons were sufficient. Being would be defined by law. Other definitions—being defined by where we live, being defined by what we do, being defined by what we were—would follow.

A short way beyond Pelagia's we crossed the road leading to the post office and Elbow Room. Set back from the beach road, its steeply pitched roof distinguished the local bar from surrounding buildings. Some afternoons and nights only a few locals were at the bar, enjoying a beer, a cup of coffee, a dance. But after vessels had docked at port loaded with golden crab, the Elbow Room lived up to its name, and nothing except the penetrating bass of the jukebox could move through the wedged crowd. Crabbing was the most dangerously driven and lucrative fishery in the world. Crew members could make more in a trip than they'd previously made in a year. But the cost was high, and every year vessels sank top-heavy with steel pots and weighted with ice. Crews on shore for a short night tried balancing money and booze against ice, exhaustion, gales, and fear. If they couldn't get into the bar, they drank on the beach. The Jug Store kept long hours. Eventually men and women, fishermen, cannery crews, and locals, unchallengeably drunk and violently in control, would careen out of the bar and into the street, making room for others. Although the population was overwhelmingly male, a madam from Kodiak found the town unprofitable and soon departed. Ice, wind, exhaustion, and fear. Booze and money. It was life at Dutch.

We passed Henry's now-shoveled walkway; the woolly dog was curled before his door. At the corner where the spruce trees stood, Anfesia and Phil turned toward the creek. I walked the opposite direction, toward the bay and home.

Aleut society was turning a corner, and like the corners on Aleut baskets the process for individuals was either active or passive. Either a third weft was added, making a deliberate corner row that forced the warp downward or nothing was added, and under tight stitches, the gradually increasing circumference turned. That is, corners were turned by adding or not adding, by doing or by not doing. In either case, tension on the weft was critical and resulted in a new direction to the weaving. Both methods worked, but for beginning weavers the use of local grass, Native grass, was essential. The imported raffia was too strong a fiber and the beginning weaver would never learn the correct tension required for a smooth transfer of direction.

I began to realize that by learning to weave, I would eventually give up weaving. What right had I to practice this craft?

Turning the corner with the addition of a third weft strand is known as the Attu corner, because it was often found on baskets made by weavers from that island. The gently curved corner produced without a third weft was characteristic of many baskets from Atka. Unalaska weavers, hopelessly eclectic, used both methods and occasionally even made sharp corners without the three-weft row. Anfesia described the Attu corner this way:

> *Turning the corner, Attu-style. When the corner is to be turned, a third weft (C) must be added. Add this weft in the same way that new warp are inserted. The result is that two wefts (A and C) are on the outside top and one weft (B) is underneath, wrapped through the fingers of the left hand. Of the two wefts on the top, although they are next to each other one (A) is further to the left. In weaving the next stitch a warp is brought over. This is properly done with the thumb of the left hand so that the right hand can maintain tension on the wefts (A and C). A stitch is now twined using the weft which is underneath (B) and the weft which is further to the left (A)—in effect passing over the other weft (C) in order to twine the warp. This produces a stitch which is slightly longer than regular weaving, and this gives Attu corners their distinctive appearance. The secret here as elsewhere is to twist the weft tightly and to keep an even tension on them. The result now is that weft A is underneath, and wefts C and B are on top. The next exchange will be between wefts C and A. This process continues on around until the beginning stitch is reached. The shortest weft is dropped out, and weaving continues with the two longer strands. On the next round, the third weft is tucked under and later it is cut off.*

If Unalaska was not yet my home, it was a place where I saw myself reflected or which I imagined was reflected in me: walking alone across the shoals of an autumn alpine valley, pausing before a steep summer descent through ferns and grass to watch the sea slide toward the shore like a green tray, surrendering to wind, balanced at an unnatural angle, the gusts bucking above the numbing mean velocity. But four years—six counting the years in the army—is a very short time, even for someone in his late twenties, and I was presumptuous to claim any legitimate connection with this place.

Throughout my absence I had kept tied to the island by threads of wild rye. When I came home, the crab fishery had burgeoned, the town doubled and tripled in size. It began to resemble a displaced panic-stricken suburb of Seattle. Pickups, trucks, and cars had reclaimed the roads. (Carol Moller's old dog Aleut, however, continued to sleep in the middle of the street, oblivious of traffic swerving around him.) The city council began zoning property: heavy industrial, commercial, residential. The surplus of garbage and the dearth of piped fresh water became critical issues. Homeless, jobless transients knocked at doors.

One afternoon during the fall I returned, I was hiking into town from the south side of the lake where I'd been picking blueberries and collecting a few blades of basket grass. A flock of seagulls huddled on the shore. My eyes focused on something larger in their midst: an emperor goose. I laughed at the thought that the goose considered itself hidden, but then I realized that with hundreds of those regal birds at the entrance to Summer Bay, no one would bother a flock of gulls for one old goose.

However welcomed I felt now in homes at Unalaska, I knew I was still a stranger. It might be said I was like the goose hiding among seagulls, but the Unalaska Aleuts were not seagulls. They were *qawalangin*, people toward the east. The similarity of that name to the word for sea lion, *qawax̂*, allowed them to become, like the six sons of *Agalinax̂*, sea lions themselves.

Like the goose, I took shelter in the things I did. I wove baskets. I scraped and blew soaked sea lion intestines to make the clear, pliable material for wallbags and raincoats. I ate the salted raw humps from the backs of freshly snagged pink salmon. I spread salmon caviar—bright roe, chopped onions, seasoned with pepper—on fresh bread. I dipped a little bread in seal oil and felt the oil coat my mouth and throat like a rush of sour mint.

Anfesia invited me to a special tea for the elders Bill and Polly McGlashan of Akutan. She had me over to meet a visiting priest, the bishop welcomed by bells. I was invited to the priest's, my *atcha*'s, for tea after the midnight New Year's service. I picked yards and yards of

, a long-running green plant, for Anfesia to use in decorat-
urch for Easter. Father Gromoff's wife asked me to come
for Easter breakfast at three or four in the morning—whether or not
I chose to endure the hours of service that preceded it. When I
arrived at Anfesia's at eleven that night, ready to attend service, she
told me to go home, set an alarm clock, and get some sleep.

But whether we were immigrants, transients, old-timers, or
locals—people who lived in the Aleutians were never in doubt about
their place in the world. We were never in control. The sea overpow-
ered everyone. We all knew perpetual earthquakes slept beneath the
bare, enfolding mountains. Everyone, one time or another, had been
swallowed alive by wind.

## 11

# A Spring Hike

As I left town carrying my pack and sleeping bag, I noticed grass edging the road. Green had seeped into the town's few lawns and elsewhere peeked out of shaggy clumps of dried weeds. From a shoulder of the mountain behind Agamgik Bay, I saw green had climbed into the lower hills like a slowly rising flood. It had covered the lips of the valley and spread upward across the belly of the pass leading to English Bay. I was in search of wild garlic, and it was spring, the Aleutians' most elusive season.

Early spring is buried when late winter dumps record amounts of snow in mid-April. The snow that melts the snow—to use a favorite phrase of Sophie Sherebernikoff—drifts down in May or early June and suddenly it is summer. When the botanist Hulten arrived on May 1, 1932, expecting to collect plants, he found there were no visible signs that the growing period had started. However, there is a spring in late May or early June, the time of white anemones, a moment of white flowers. White anemones and deep yellow marsh marigolds on succulent green stalks. Along the road to the dump or at the cemetery or near the lake, orchids sprout from nothingness. Clusters of purple and red blossom on thick stems. Their taller skinnier cousins, white bog orchids, grow nearby: some without any scent, some with heaven's gift.

English Bay had received its name after the summer of 1778 when James Cook and his crew aboard the *Resolution* and *Discovery* anchored there twice. Entering the narrow harbor at the northeast corner of Beaver Inlet in thick treacherous fog, Cook expressed his thankfulness at escaping shipwreck by naming his anchorage Providence Bay. However, upon learning that Aleuts called the bay Samganooda, he afterward used this local name. Locals, Aleuts and Russians, however, frequently referred to Samganooda as English Bay in recognition of his visit. Following a brief stay in June, Cook returned to spend most of September anchored in the protective harbor. Although some of the crew slept aboard the *Discovery*, others established a camp on shore while the *Resolution*, which had developed severe leaks, was partially resided and recaulked.

Journals kept by Cook, Samwell, Edgar, and others reveal a crew thoroughly relishing the delights of an Aleutian summer. The fishing was easy, and in three or four hours the men could "fill their boats with holybut of an enormous size" at the mouth of the harbor. They caught salmon, picked berries, and enjoyed the vigorous company of local women.

The uninhibited frankness of these late eighteenth-century journals contrasts dramatically with the pinched righteousness in journals from a century later. John Ledyard, an American corporal, volunteered to accompany Aleuts to the Russian settlement at Iliuliuk. The head of the garrison, Ismailov, visited Cook aboard ship where the two men quizzed each other on new geographical discoveries—as much as no common language could allow. Cook's artist, John Webber, drew portraits of a man and woman and sketched the interior and exterior of an Aleut *barabara*; all four works eventually were transferred to engravings and widely circulated. In his journal Cook referred to "baskets of grass which are both strong and beautiful."

Reaching the head of Agamgik Bay about noon, I stashed my pack and sleeping bag on a grassy bank away from the water. Carrying a day pack, I left the beach following a creek inland. Struggling through tangled fallen beach grass, I surprised a young mallard swimming in the narrow stream, but after giving me a nervous glance it merely paddled a little quicker and disappeared around a bend. Like the creek leading into Ugadaga, this one was serpentine, and to avoid repeated crossings I stayed far to the right at the base of the gradually rising hills. Once the low summit of the pass was reached, the way led across fields until a small but spectacular inland waterfall brought me back to the creek. I stopped for a drink and noticed a growth of saxifrage close to the stream. A gradual descent led to a beach of black sand and rough rocks littered with oyster shells. Sculpted eagle feathers lay among blades of grass. Across the creek a red fox, gracelessly shrugging off its winter coat, slipped out of sight.

I followed the narrow shoreline on the left until my way was blocked by a cliff that dropped into deep water. I studied the cliff for a fine, short grass Anfesia said could be stuffed into socks to keep the feet warm and dry, and prevent frostbite in the winter. It was very effective as a filter for cold air when wadded up and placed in the mouth. Because it was so fine, it could be dried out by rubbing it between the palms and then used to get a fire going.

Backtracking a little, I climbed up and into Vasilii Shaishnikoff's long-abandoned homesite, where Andrew Makarin had told Anfesia that wild onions could be smelled.

Vasilii Shaishnikoff was born around 1859, a son of Father Innokentii Shaishnikoff and his wife, Maria. Several of the children of this notable Aleut priest and his wife played important roles in the community following his death in 1883. Vasilii was elected chief of the community a few years later when local people ignored the chief appointed by the Alaska Commercial Company and selected their own leader. He traveled to Nome during the 1900 gold rush, along with thousands of would-be prospectors who had littered the shores of Dutch Harbor waiting for the northern ice to clear. His older brother Alexander was an agent for the Alaska Commercial Company at Atka and Attu.

Both Vasilii and his brother Alexander eventually settled outside of Unalaska village. Alexander—Sasha—homesteaded at the head of Captain's Bay and Vasilii filed for a 160-acre homestead site in English Bay in 1908, although he probably had been living there off and on for many years. Henry remarked that Vasilii was said to have lived there for forty-two years. This bay had the only mackerel grounds around Unalaska, and Vasilii caught them and put them up in kegs for sale to the A.C. Company. Vasilii also had a house in Unalaska, where he spent most summers working as a carpenter. Both Shaishnikoff brothers were excellent gardeners, as had their father been before them, and Vasilii grew potatoes, turnips, and other vegetables in an area with excellent drainage and sunlight.

If Vasilii himself brought the garlic to English Bay, he probably did so before 1910 when he returned from Attu, where for a short time he served as agent for the Alaska Commercial Company. Around 1930, Henry was passing English Bay and stopped in. Vasilii caught a ride to Unalaska, where he became ill. Anfesia said her first husband, Deacon Michael Tutiakoff, had prepared Vasilii's last will before his own death in 1933.

Nail-studded boards, two rusted saws, and a few pieces of iron were all that remained of the frame house perched above the cliff. By 1927 this house had replaced the original *barabara* that Vasilii had constructed and which Henry Swanson had visited: "He had a nice *barabara*, wallpaper and all that inside. It was like a house, but it was made out of sods instead of lumber."

I gazed over the knee-high vegetation for any signs of cultivation. Nothing. Only slightly hopeful, I began walking through the plants, crushing leaves with my hands and smelling them for any traces of onion or garlic. Apart from "broad leaves and reticulate covering on the bulbs," I had found no descriptions of *Allium evictorialis*. I knew enough not to crush the elephantine leaves of *putchkii, Heracleum lanatum,* in my bare hands and to avoid the even more potent low *putchkii.* I knew that wormwood, *Artemisia unalaskensis,* wasn't what I wanted, but I loved its smoky scent. After fifteen minutes of picking, shredding, and sniffing an assortment of plants, I moved away from the campsite over toward a slanting hillside that terminated on the beach.

As I worked my way across, leaving a trail of ravaged plants, I remembered Anfesia had told me that as a girl she was sent to collect a fern that stayed green all winter. Sore muscles were relieved when soaked in hot water containing the leaves and roots of this plant. She said she was scolded when she pleaded ignorance of this plant and expressed doubt that anything green could be found growing in the blizzard that had started to blow. She went out to the side of the hill where she had been instructed to go. There, nestled in snow, were clumps of *qaalmiidan.*

Anfesia's first theory was that Vasilii Shaishnikoff himself had transplanted the garlic, but she suggested another possibility: that George Washington had brought the garlic to please the Rock of Ages. The great weaver Vassa Prokopeuff was married to Anfesia's uncle, Phileret Prokopeuff, chief of Attu. He and four other men had mysteriously disappeared on the south side of Attu in 1910. After her husband's death, Maggie—as Vassa was called—supported herself by weaving. She loved to dance and made occasional trips to Unalaska where ready dance partners were more available. Crews from visiting Coast Guard cutters purchased her basketry and supplied a dancing partner or two. Neither her love of dance nor her excellent weaving ever diminished, and she earned the nickname Rock of Ages.

When Vassa Prokopeuff arrived at Unalaska for another visit around 1926, she brought a blind woman and her daughter Jenny, as well as her late husband's godson, George Golodoff, nicknamed George Washington. George spent much time with Vasilii at English Bay. He also made several trips back to Attu on various occasions. On one of these trips, he brought his younger brother, Innokentii Golodoff, to stay with Maggie. Anfesia speculated that he may also have brought wild garlic to Unalaska. Anfesia recalled Maggie saying how she wished she had some *chermitchen* to eat with her food. And whenever she got some, Anfesia remembered, she would nibble on the mild-tasting stems as on a green onion.

About seventy-five yards northeast of the Shaishnikoff campsite, I saw a clump about six feet in diameter of unusually wide-leafed plants. Water trickled around the patch, and monkey faces bloomed in the damp soil. Smooth, reddish buds arched on long stems curving out of tulip-like leaves. I quickly broke one of the buds in my hands and inhaled the broad triumphant odor of garlic.

From the oval of garlic on the hillside, I looked northeast along the narrow bay toward its entrance at Fisherman's Point. A small army outpost had been erected there by the time of white flowers in 1942, the time when war erupted over Beaver Inlet.

On June 4, 1942, a PBY, the slow but sure workhorse aircraft of the Aleutian Campaign, lumbered its way from Cold Bay to Unalaska with mail and a crew of seven, while thirty-one Japanese planes skirted the southern side of Unalaska Island, crossed over Beaver Inlet, and headed across Unalga Pass. The PBY was no match for the Zeros that peeled off the formation and sent the American plane flaming into the water off Egg Island. It was a little after five-thirty in the afternoon, and the Japanese planes continued on to Dutch Harbor for a second day of attacks. Henry Swanson tended outposts in Beaver Inlet, and a short time later he delivered supplies to the post at Fisherman's Point, where he heard about the downing of the plane and the deaths of the crew. The survivors of the fiery plunge had scrambled into a life raft and had begun paddling ashore when another Zero swept down, strafing the raft and killing all aboard.

Although an attack on Dutch Harbor had been anticipated, when the Kate bombers and Zeros descended out of the overcast skies over the village at 5:50 A.M. on June 3, people were indeed surprised. Japanese bombs struck army barracks in Margaret Bay where twenty-five men were killed, the majority of the thirty-five killed during the two days of attack. Four waves of attack on June 3 were followed by more that began at about 6 P.M. on June 4. During the second attack, 22,000 barrels of fuel oil ignited when steel tanks were hit. Rolling clouds darkened the skies for days. No local residents were injured. There had been air raid practices prior to the attack, and locals had scurried to shelters when they heard the Klaxon blaring. The east side of the Bureau of Indian Affairs hospital was demolished when a bomb dropped beside it, but the patients had been taken to bunkers. The Church of the Holy Ascension escaped bombs and strafing.

After Pearl Harbor, the wives and children of military personnel or civilian workers employed by the military had been sent away from Unalaska. Random and uncoordinated discussions were held among the Army, the Navy, the Office of Indian Affairs, the Fish and Wildlife Service, and the Division of Territories and Island Possessions about the safety of Aleuts in the Aleutian and Pribilof Islands, but not those living on the Alaska Peninsula. Numerous proposals were suggested and discussions continued through June 17, even though the Navy had evacuated and burned Atka village on June 12 and evacuated the Pribilof Islands on June 16.

At Unalaska, packing church valuables was a community effort that began a month before the actual order for evacuation was issued. The day the Pribilof Island people boarded the *Delarof*, Chief William Zaharoff and three men—Peter Galaktionoff, Peter Samakunsky, and John Gordeiff—packed the first box of church belongings, while Vincent Tutiakoff recorded the inventory. The next day as the eighty-three Atka residents transferred aboard the *Delarof*, now docked at Unalaska and already crowded with the 477 Pribilof Islanders, Father Dionecious removed items from the altar as Vincent Tutiakoff once again took inventory. On June 18, as the *Delarof* sailed for an unknown destination, Zaharoff and his three men were joined by Joe Chagin, William Dyakanoff, Walter Dyakanoff, Tim Tutiakoff, and Tracy Tutiakoff, and a third box of church belongings was crated, again inventoried by Vincent Tutiakoff. These inventories, now in the Church of the Holy Ascension, indicate that Vincent was Chairman and Recording Secretary of the Unalaska Church Committee. In her position as Reader, Anfesia packed boxes of church service books. She recalled taking sixteen cartons of books with her to the desolation that was Southeast Alaska.

On July 5, 1942, Nikolski was evacuated and soon joined by the last residents of Biorka, Kashega, Makushin, and a few people working at Chernofski. On July 19, the SS *Alaska* arrived at Unalaska to evacuate Aleuts residing there. Although an evacuation was expected, people were actually given only twenty-four hours to prepare for departure. Each person was allowed only one suitcase of belongings. Mothers dressed their children in several layers of clothes. Every family was forced to leave valuable heirlooms behind: icons, samovars, and albums of photographs. Anfesia hated leaving Michael Tutiakoff's violin, but things were hidden as well as possible. The doors were shut and locked. By July 26, 1942, the 881 Aleuts who had lived in villages west of Unimak Island had left the Aleutians.

Until late August 1942, the only village still inhabited by Aleuts was the one on Attu Island, but their village had been occupied by Japanese forces. Attu had been the first Aleutian Island to experience the oppression of the West when the crew of a Russian vessel commanded by Mikhail Nevodchikov wintered there in 1745-1746. For two hundred years the Attuans had survived as a unique branch of the Aleut people. Near the end of August, the forty-one residents of the village were ordered aboard a coal freighter and taken away from their island. In 1945, the twenty-five survivors of the internment on Hokkaido made the long journey to Tokyo (Atsugi), Okinawa, Manila, San Francisco, Seattle, and finally back to Alaska—to Atka Island, but never again to home.

After the Attuans departed for Japan, only a handful of Aleut civilians remained in the islands: men like Henry Swanson, who worked for the military, and John Yatchmenef, Chief Alexei's son, who worked for the Seims Drake construction firm and stayed behind to help safeguard the church. In addition, Aleut men had volunteered for military service and others had been drafted; a small group of these served in the Aleutians.

The Aleut inhabitation of the islands which had been continuous for over eight thousand years lay in the hands of these few men.

Using my hands and pocketknife, I dug up a sturdy clump of wild garlic and wrapped the roots in a plastic bag. After crossing the gradual pass from English Bay to Agamgik, I collected my backpack and sleeping bag and headed for the Quonset hut at the mouth of Agamgik Bay. With the garlic carefully nestled in an elbow of the rivulet running behind the hut, I started a fire in the old barrel stove and prepared for night. Darkness was slow to arrive. The nearly cloudless sky provided an almost endless arc of light from one day to another.

Early June, late May, mixed the promises of spring with bitter memories of the evacuation to Southeast Alaska. There Aleuts lived under deplorable conditions in a country where tangled forests obscured the sky, where trees dripped on them and made the evening unnaturally dark. At home their houses fell prey to the ravages of weather and to looting by American servicemen and civilian construction workers. By the time they were allowed to return, three years after the bombing, two years after the cessation of hostilities in the Chain, they had buried many of their elders in the soggy southeastern soil. Upon arriving at Unalaska on April 22, 1945, people were corralled in military buildings on the slopes of Mount Newhall. Anfesia's twenty-one-year-old son, Tracy, and a few other adventurous young people sneaked by the military police, climbed over the barbed wire strung around the village, and walked through town as far as the dock. They returned with news that most homes were now uninhabitable.

The community insisted they be allowed to return to their homes, where almost every family found objects of value and memory destroyed or missing: icons, photographs, clothing, hunting equipment, an old violin. They had to argue with authorities for permission to hold a funeral service in the church for Ma Newell. A feisty woman who had been born in Biorka around 1876, Martha Newell had died at the end of February 1945 after soliciting a promise that she would be taken home for burial.

The first job was to find places to live, and then on June 7, Anfesia made time to draft letters for the church committee. One went to the U. S. Commissioner who had rented church property to various parties. The committee wanted an accounting of the rent money and of church papers left in his care by the chief. Church committee members had tried to see him but the commissioner had skipped town. Another letter was addressed to the Metropolitan, informing him of their return and expressing concerns over church funds and rental property and wondering what to do about a missing antimins—a cloth essential to the celebration of Divine Liturgy. The church was in need of immediate repairs. Chief Alexei Yatchmenef's son John had drowned during the time people were in Southeast Alaska and the care of the church was neglected by authorities.

The U.S. Commissioner had written to William Zaharoff in March 1945 that the siding of the church had been damaged during a storm and that the roof was now leaking. Without continual vigilance, the integrity of any building in the Aleutians is compromised by persistent wind and rain.

Once again the maintenance of the church building and the holding of services devolved on local parishioners. Father Dionecious did not return. Occasional visits were made to Unalaska by the priest from St. Paul Island, Father Makary Baranoff. He was a generous, humble man who towered above the members of his congregation. He had accompanied the Pribilof Islanders during their evacuation and had returned to serve them after the war.

On June 8, 1947, Anfesia's eldest son, Vincent, drowned. He had been celebrating and fell from a skiff into one of the few deep holes in the creek that runs beside the church. He was twenty-five years old. If John Yatchmenef and Vincent Tutiakoff had lived, the recovery of Aleut communities after the war might have been quicker and more organized. Both men had been trained by their respective parents to serve as leaders. At twenty, Vincent had already been an officer in the Orthodox Brotherhood. During the war he served in the military and on one occasion assisted his stranded companions with knowledge of Aleut survival skills.

The years in Southeast Alaska, however, had so shredded Aleut communal life that it is probable even these two men, energetic, literate, and intelligent, could not have restored it to its former shape and pattern. In any event, their deaths were but layers in the grief facing Aleuts after the war.

Anfesia herself became ill and the doctors said she had but a short time to live.

I found Anfesia sitting at her kitchen table splitting weaves and weavers (warp and weft strands) from blades of grass. Using the second blades, not the very inners which were reserved strictly for weft fibers, she would make two wefts from the outside of a blade and then strip off another strand from each side for two warp strands. The entire stock of warp and weft needed for a basket were prepared before weaving began.

"*Aang*, Qumatu," she said as I carried in the plants and set them in the sink. She felt the long wide leaves and smiled as the faint garlic odor crossed to her fingers. She cleared off part of the table, being careful to keep the two piles of split grass separate. As she poured me a cup of tea and added a little hot water to her cup, she said, "Guess who I got a letter from?" I had no idea and soon she showed me an envelope with a Japanese stamp.

"Bishop Vladimir," she said quietly, delight and sorrow in those two words.

An American, he was the Orthodox Bishop of Japan residing at the Orthodox cathedral in Tokyo, but on October 16, 1960, he had arrived at Unalaska as a young priest, Father Basil Nagosky. Three months later poor health forced him to return to New York and Anfesia had noted in her diary, "He was with us three months and left, but he has done three to ten years work here for the church as well as for the children." Then she had added, "So keep up the good work." He returned for Easter that spring and remained until May 2, 1962, when he was elevated to bishop and sent to Japan. He had been the first resident priest since World War II, and he had reinvigorated the community. For his parishioners his transfer had felt like a personal attack, and they had protested in a vigorous letter to the head of the church in America, Metropolitan Leonti. Once again services would depend upon visiting clergy and Aleut lay persons: John Golodoff, Andrew Makarin, John Tcheripanoff, Anfesia.

In Vietnam I had wanted to take my R&R at the coldest spot available, and in December that was Japan. With Anfesia's encouragement I had knocked at a side door of the great stone Japanese cathedral, Nikolai Do. The housekeeper had called Bishop Vladimir (Basil Nagosky), who looked at me curiously until I said I had brought greetings from Anfesia Shapsnikoff. He welcomed me in for tea. He asked about many of his former parishioners, people for whom he had not only fondness and love, but also the deepest respect.

"He's lonesome for the Aleutians," Anfesia said. "With eleven million people and he is lonely. I can't understand it, but I think he is like you. He has his heart set for Unalaska."

I did not read his letter. After she laid it aside, her hand returned to touch it again.

That afternoon Anfesia and I transplanted a small patch of Vasilii's garlic to the head of Unalaska Lake. We hoped it would develop, but Anfesia was skeptical. An attempt to grow it at Captain's Bay had failed. She remembered that Kiriaka Popoff, an old man from Biorka, had tried transplanting some to that village, but because Andrew Makarin had never mentioned them, she thought the plants had not survived. Before we left her house, however, she brought a knife and a cutting board to the table, and joining the ghost of the Rock of Ages, we two savored the mingled flavors of mild garlic and green onion.

## 12
# Village Lives, Village Friendships

I arrived at Anfesia's for tea and found the kitchen filled with food: baked ham and turkey, mashed potatoes, homemade bread, real butter, salmonberry jelly, fried *alaadiks*, slices of carrots and celery, creamed corn served cold, fish pie made with silver salmon, bowls of sweet pickles and olives and sliced smoked salmon tasting like autumn. Then Sophie Sherebernikoff and her daughter Jenny carried in a Jell-O salad, a macaroni salad, a loaf of fresh bread, and coleslaw. Mary Robinson and her mother, Agnes Chagin, brought two cakes and a blueberry pie. Marina, Anfesia's daughter-in-law, proudly delivered a sea lion roast. A kitchen full of kerchiefed women wearing dark dresses wielded pot holders and knives as Aleut and English ricocheted off the walls.

Father Gromoff, who had stayed at church to hear confessions, arrived last, and as he came into the living room, we all stood. It was a very special day as he crossed himself before the family icon and greeted everyone. As he made his way around the room a voice at the kitchen doorway said, "Holy! It's about time!" and everyone laughed as Mother Gromoff feigned surprise at seeing her husband. Then she saw me and said, "*Aang, ugix̂. Where's your brot?*"

"I think he went upstairs," I said and in a moment Anfesia's son Phil came down.

"Mother's looking for you," I said. "I think they're ready."

Phil asked Father if he would bless the food. People crowded into the kitchen and faced the icon of St. Nicholas as Father gave a short grace and led the singing in Russian of the Lord's Prayer. We were to take food from the table and sit in the living room or in chairs placed around the kitchen. Father was asked to go in line first, followed by Nick, the church warden, and all the men. We made our way into the living room with plates heaping with food. Sophie came around with tea and coffee. Gradually we were joined by women, but Anfesia and Sophie continued to hover around the kitchen, slicing meat and fish pie, filling bowls with more mashed potatoes and vegetables and gravy.

When at last Anfesia came in to sit down, Ben Golodoff got up and gave her his seat.

"You don't have to do that," she said.

"You've been working hard," he replied and made himself comfortable on the floor.

Anfesia sat down next to Mrs. Makarin, Andrew's sister-in-law, and said, "I can remember days when Mrs. Makarin and I would row a boat to Summer Bay and get wood."

At that Mrs. Chagin smiled at Anfesia and Mrs. Makarin and said, "Those days are gone, Pal. If we got in a boat now, we'd drift away!"

People laughed and Anfesia said, "Many of times I try to teach people what they need to know to survive if they get shipwrecked."

"Good thing, too!" teased Phil and Anfesia shook her finger at him. "You don't even know what to look for on the beach," she scolded.

"The first thing I'd look for," Phil said, "is a grocery store!"

"Remind me not to go out with you again," Father said jokingly. I looked at Mother Gromoff and we both laughed. "Once was enough."

"Criminey! I thought you knew how to handle a skiff."

"What do you mean?" Father said. "Unalaska people are supposed to be the good boat handlers!"

The story of the trip that Father, Mother, Phil, and I had taken in a skiff from the creek to the sand spit at Dutch didn't need retelling. Our first mistake, other than getting into the skiff, was to rev the engine as we went under the dock pilings and almost knock off the oars. The wind had risen by the time we were ready to come back from our picnic, and we'd been rescued by someone with a more seaworthy skiff.

"You guys! With Father and Mother? Shame on you!" This from Sophie Sherebernikoff. And she meant it.

Anfesia continued supervising my weaving. She had me make a small utilitarian basket, a fish basket, distinguished by the open weave found in matting. I stretched it over a pound coffee tin to keep its shape, but when I braided the top edge, I pulled too tightly and the sides warped with a gathered wrinkle. She continued to give me information about Aleut culture, and I dutifully took notes.

> Mrs. Shapsnikoff said that for an Aleut feast when she was a child, the table would be set with three main things: fish pie, salted whole small trout, and burned flour. To prepare the burned flour it was cooked on the stove in a frying pan without any oil or lard, just dry, or it could be baked in the oven until thoroughly brown. This loose flour was then mixed in a cup with hot water or tea. It could be made the consistency of pudding and eaten plain or with butter and salt.

On a hike back from Summer Bay I had found a wooden mallet-like object on the trail. I thought it might be something used for mashing potatoes that had washed ashore from a passing vessel and been found by a hiker and tossed on the trail. When I showed it to Anfesia, however, she said it was an old basket form. It was, basically, a cylinder about five inches long with a four-inch diameter and with a short handle and knob on one end. Baskets were not woven around these, but were stretched over them when at rest to assure a uniform shape. I never discovered how this artifact—certainly dating from before the war—landed on the ground before me. I imagined a red fox unearthing it from its lair or Maggie Prokopeuff hurling it from heaven.

> *Aleut medicines: For a headache resulting from a concussion, the hair is pulled away from the back of the head, and a needle of some sort is gouged in and blood let out. For pains around the heart, a strip of cloth is tied above the chest, under the arms. With a knife made from the tooth of a large black fish, the two veins under the side of the tongue are cut, the tongue being turned over and held against the teeth. This relieves the condition. Sergie Sovoroff knows all of this in detail and Mrs. Shapsnikoff hopes to learn more from him.*
>
> *Some part of the swan was used for medicine. Swans used to be found on the south side of the island, in Beaver Inlet. Nick Shaishnikoff's grandfather was a great hunter, and once he was caught in bad weather and had to leave his baidarka at English Bay and walk overland to get home. On this occasion Mrs. Shapsnikoff saw her first swan when he returned to the village with it.*

Although Anfesia had shown me the way Attu weaving differed from other Aleut weaving, it was not until she thought I was proficient with the Unalaska technique that she gave me instructions. Although two weft strands are used, in Attu weaving the bottom weft is twined through the fingers of the left hand and thus is under or inside the basket. The top weft is, of course, on the outside. When twining a stitch, the new warp strand is moved into place by the thumb of the left hand. The top weft is brought down, across the warp, and exchanged with the weft which is underneath. The exchange is made by straightening the left hand's middle finger. This releases the weft, which is then picked up by the middle finger of the right hand which reaches in, catches it, and draws it up while the top weft, held by the thumb and index finger of the right hand, is slipped into its place among the fingers of the left hand.

The weft that was originally on the bottom is now held in the bent middle finger of the right hand and brought up to the top where it is picked up by the right hand's thumb and index finger. This exchange can be done without any loss of tension and so the weaving remains tight.

The days of early June and late May, the season of white flowers, recalled the time of greatest loss for Unalaska Aleuts in this century, surpassing even the events of the war. Five days of cloudless sunny weather had unfolded last February, and on one of those days I went over to Anfesia's. Agnes Chagin was also visiting, and out of the blue Mrs. Chagin said, "This is unhealthy weather." I raised my eyebrows in surprise, and Anfesia said, "This is the way the weather was during the 1919 flu. Everything was so still and quiet—no wind at all."

Although the stormy Aleutian weather is eager to provide appropriate pathetic fallacies for tragedies, those days between May 26 and June 13, 1919, when forty-four people died, were days of calm and sunshine. In the evening after lowering the flag, men from the Revenue Cutter Service would go from house to house, collect the dead bodies, and bury them in long trenches. Anfesia's mother, Martha Lazarev, had been ill since February, but she survived until June 6. After her only four more died. The last, Anfesia recalled, was a woman visiting from St. Paul. The outbreak had been so fierce and sudden, utterly paralyzing the community, that only this last death was followed by a funeral in the church. The epidemic had also taken Anfesia's aunt and basketry teacher, Mary Levigne.

Anfesia and others continued to remember the victims of that epidemic. Her diary notes that on Sunday, June 5, 1966, she attended church. After the service she and others removed the decorations which had been up for the forty days after Easter, and then she went to Walter and Mrs. Moller's for lunch. Later in the afternoon, she returned to church with her grandson Vince and held a brief service, a memorial service for the victims of that long-ago flu and for her dead son.

Like the oklad, an icon's gilded covering that focused attention on the essential truth of the painting, what Anfesia did illumined her character. As Aleuts and Russians of the Far East had shared much in their ancient pre-literate culture, so now they shared a common Christian tradition. Through this Orthodox culture, Anfesia participated in a religious and literate tradition that extended back over a thousand years. Part of this Orthodox tradition promoted the use of Native languages. In Alaska, local languages were not only valued but they were provided with written scripts by early Orthodox missionaries and converts. Aleut was the first such language to receive an alphabet.

Anfesia made several translations into Aleut of Bahá'í prayers and quotations for me. I think she did this because she wanted me to have in her language something that was of importance to me. It was a gesture of great kindness.

In the spring of 1967, I had been trying to translate a short prayer when Anfesia handed me a knife and a peeled onion. She was making fish pie.

"Here, slice this," she said, "and I'll translate." Before entering the army that fall I sent her translation to the Bahá'í World Center in Haifa, Israel. She wrote, "I received your letter, a welcome one, and I have thought of it many times. . . . I feel unworthy to be known in such a place as the Holy Land. . . . When Addie and I sat and talked about my boys and you and other people I would get the heavy burden off of me. . . . But that Lucky piece of paper to be in Holy Land. But you sent it there. Thank you. *Txin angunasix qaĝaasakuqing* [I thank you very much.]"

Her willingness to do this for me sprang from the same source as another act. When I was in Vietnam she wrote to tell me her grandson Vincent would soon be stationed there.

"I have a candle burning for you both," she wrote, "so you are remembered in our prayers."

When I expressed concern that translating material might cause her problems with people in the village, she said, "I used to worry about what they thought of my friends, but I don't anymore."

In 1966 I had requested permission to make a pilgrimage to the Bahá'í World Center, and in 1970 I was invited to spend nine days visiting the gardens and shrines on the slopes of Mount Carmel and on the plain of Akka. The Persian government had banished Bahá'u'lláh and his family to Iraq in 1863 and subsequent extensions of the exile brought them to Palestine in 1868. Eventually he was able to move into rented quarters outside the prison city of Akka. In one of these homes he spent the last years of his life, and there he died in 1892 and was buried. The purpose of a pilgrimage is to visit the Shrine of Bahá'u'lláh at Bahji and the Shrine of the Báb, Bahá'u'lláh's forerunner, on Mount Carmel. After the Báb was executed in Tabriz in 1850, his remains were rescued from the edge of a moat where they had been cast and kept in hiding until they were interred on Mount Carmel in 1909. Beautiful gardens have been crafted around these two sites sacred to Bahá'ís, and there I visited from July 6 to July 15.

I had left Unalaska June 5, on a morning when low clouds muted the landscape, obscuring the shape of the island. At the corner of Unalaska Bay, Priest Rock stood above dark water like a solid shadow. In Norway I strolled through an Oslo garden filled with sensually spiritual sculptures by Gustav Vigeland. In Bergen I saw the portrait of my grandmother's uncle, Domprovst Carsten Hansteen, hanging in a vast church. In London I went to see several Aleut hats collected by Captain Cook on display in the British Museum. After the days in Haifa, since I would be already halfway around the world, I continued my trip eastward to Alaska with stops in Iran, India, and Vietnam. In Iran, I was able to visit Shiraz, a city of graceful trees and poetry whose heart was a small house where an ancient well and an orange tree filled a small enclosed courtyard. The house of the Báb would be destroyed as persecutions rivaling those that occurred under the various shahs began to afflict the Bahá'ís of Iran in the 1980s and 1990s, but in 1970 I sat in the shade of the orange tree and visited the upstairs room where my religion had its beginning. Back in Teheran, I purchased two small, old, brass samovars, one for my mother and one for Anfesia.

The highlight of my trip to India was receiving a letter Anfesia had sent in care of the National Spiritual Assembly of the Bahá'ís of India. She wrote that she was working on the final border of a basket.

She and Lois Hope had picked grass and it was about ready to be separated into individual blades. As I lay under a slowly revolving ceiling fan in sweltering heat, I read how Unalaska's weather in early July had been like October's—"It's so cold it's not even funny"—and people were bundling up to go outside. The Fourth of July celebration had been moved into the school gym. One of the children removed by the state social worker years ago was expected back, but whether to stay or only for a visit, no one knew.

Anfesia hadn't smoked or salted fish for three years, so she was hoping to spend time at Nick Shaishnikoff's camp when the weather improved. Her friend from Cold Bay, Dorothy Jones, had been in town collecting things for the university museum.

"Seems like they are just now finding that there are Aleuts around here," she wrote.

My little *atcha*, Jimmy Krukoff, had been over to see her three times, but she had had another argument with my silent *atcha*, Father Gromoff. She had also tangled with a storekeeper and accused him of selling alcohol to someone on probation. He in turn had accused her of trying to shut down his business through a conspiracy with Robin Fowler, the city manager and a good friend of mine. A new policeman had been hired, and he seemed better than the last one who had arrived one day, spent two days standing on the beach staring at the Bering Sea, and skipped town on the next available plane.

I spent six days in Saigon visiting Bahá'ís and renewing a friendship with a young Buddhist with whom I had corresponded since 1968. During the year I was stationed in Vietnam, I was told the capital city was off limits, and so everything now was new except the music of that beautiful language: all the bright signs, the gaudy taxis, the crowded streets displaying the worst public statues ever erected. I ate a superb French meal in a glass-enclosed restaurant high above the city and sensed that everything, even the sky, was different. There were dark clouds as before. *Then* if it rained, there was little where to go: under some strung up boards or inside a tent. But now, inside and insulated, I could not hear the wind or feel in my pores the moment the dust settled beneath the drops of rain.

I returned to Unalaska and gave Anfesia her samovar as she was preparing to leave on another trip. With its stamped, Russian double-eagle, it must have reminded her of those she saw during her childhood. World War II pillaging had emptied the village of all such mementos. Later she wrote, "I couldn't tell or explain to you at present time, cause I would only cry on your shoulder, so a small touch [will] explain it I hope. I will always cherish the samovar and fix and use it so you can see it when I get back."

"You have too many girlfriends!" she scolded and slammed her hand on the table. "You don't spend any time in my house! I wanted to give you some bread, but you didn't even stay long enough!"

Anfesia was at her table having a cup of tea. Three days before she had not been feeling well when I came for a visit, and so I had just said a brief hello.

"You're feeling better today, I see."

"I'm not feeling well yet."

We had tea. I asked her if she would come to school and give a presentation to the students in the elementary grades.

"Just one visit?" she asked.

I didn't know if she wanted to visit more or if one was almost too many.

"One for now," I said. "Maybe we could arrange something more."

She told about blind Cedor Solovyov and the kind-hearted Mama Newhall and her husband, the village doctor, during the years of her childhood. "We lived like one family," she said and closed her fist to demonstrate how closely the Newhalls and the village people worked together. She pointed to the Alaska state flag with its golden Big Dipper against a dark blue sky and said Benny Benson, its designer, had been inspired by the stars he saw when he lived at Unalaska in the Jesse Lee Home. She claimed, perhaps stretching the point a little, that it had actually been designed here and not at Seward, where the home had been transferred at the time the territorial flag contest was held. She brought out a model Aleut drum and struck it while she sang two chants. She showed the class a sea lion shoulder bone.

"I've kept that because it was from the first sea lion that my grandson went and got," she said. "I kept the bone so he could show the rest of the children how the game went."

At the end of her visit she said, "There are several other things that I have that I didn't bring along. Later, maybe, I'll recuperate a little bit more, and then I can show you more and tell you more."

But later she was always too busy or we were never quite ready.

As early as 1967 Anfesia had urged me to seek funding from the state for an Aleut arts and crafts project. The draft had intervened, however, and it was not until after her visit to school that I got around to drawing up a proposal for the school board's consideration. I suggested that in the fall of 1971 Anfesia be hired to teach ten weeks of basketry, Sophie Pletnikoff to teach gut-sewing for ten weeks, and Sergie Sovoroff to give ten weeks of instruction in making model *baidarkas*. Part of the weaving class periods would be devoted to selecting, cutting, and preparing grass. Although gut prepared in the fall was inferior to that secured in the spring, Sophie's class would include basic gut preparation. If time allowed, Sergie's classes might also make fox traps or sea otter spears and throwing boards.

Both Sophie and Anfesia were available at Unalaska. I had heard that Sergie and Agnes Sovoroff were planning on returning to Unalaska to work in one of the crab canneries in the fall, and I hoped he could be talked into staying longer and teaching the class. If Sergie was unavailable, Bill Tcheripanoff of Akutan might be persuaded to teach the class. The proposal made clear that coordination of the program, which included the selection of topics and approval of the instructors, would be left to Anfesia.

Although this proposal never got off the ground, in years to come I would coordinate instruction at the school by Sophie Pletnikoff, Sergie and Agnes Sovoroff, Bill and Annie Tcheripanoff, and Augusta Dushkin. Later they would be followed by younger people such as Nick Galaktionoff, Nick Lekanoff, Ann McGlashan, and Christine Dushkin.

Late in December 1971, I sat at Anfesia's table with my tape recorder going. Anfesia reminisced about the Christmases of her childhood. She told about programs in the public school and at the Russian school and how, if weather permitted, Santa Claus would arrive on the mail boat *Dora*. She praised Dr. Newhall and his wife, Mama Newhall, who operated the Jesse Lee Home for the Methodist Church for most of the years from 1895 until 1925. She compared them with the Chief and the Second Chief in their concerns for the welfare of everyone in the community. The tape recording was transcribed and edited, and a little booklet was made which was given to each student during Russian Christmas in January 1972.

"Have some more dessert, Mr. Hudson," Sophie said, but I held up my hand and said, "Thank you, but I've had a great plenty."

"Ben? Phil? You guys, there's lots out there!"

Father said, "That seal meat was delicious. *Qaĝaasakuqing*, Marina. It makes me homesick for the islands."

"You're welcome, Father. Greg got it over by Eider Point."

"The first time Greg had a knife," Anfesia said, "he wasn't happy until his knife had the smell of seal on it. Until he had butchered his first seal."

Agnes Chagin added, "That was what the adults valued."

"But when his son got a knife," Anfesia continued, "and helped butcher a seal he was mad that it smelled that way!"

"Lots of changes."

"When I was a girl," Anfesia said, "you used to be able to drink water out of the creek. Now look at it!"

"There's even broken glass. Michael cut his foot bad that time, remember?"

"I remember John Gordeiff said seal and sea lion bones and bird bones shouldn't be tossed away. They should be buried. It's because they are just tossed out that the animals are not coming any more. They sense this, seeing the bones."

"People in those days used everything," said Pelagia McCurdy, who had spent her childhood with her grandparents living on Hog Island. "Nothing was wasted. Well, there wasn't anything to waste!"

"We need to remember these things to the children."

"There's lots of valuable things people could learn," Anfesia said.

Outside the window I saw four-year-old Vladimir playing "guns." With his wooden stick he took prone and careful aim. He fired mercilessly: Blam! His nine-year-old brother George fell backwards, deftly avoiding a rusted fifty-gallon oil barrel. Suddenly six-year-old Brenda charged out of a crumbling warehouse screeching, "Rat-a-tat-tat! You're dead, Vladimir! I got you!" Like any American kids three-quarters of the way through this scarred century.

I went back to Anfesia's a half-hour after I had left, thinking most of the people would have gone and I could help clean up. Phil had joined Peter and Laresa over on Amaknak. Agnes Chagin and Sophie Sherebernikoff were helping Anfesia finish up in the kitchen when I entered.

"*Aang, aang!*" Anfesia said and told me to sit at the table which had been moved back against the wall.

"*Chaayuda,* Mr. Hudson?" Sophie asked and brought me a cup of tea without waiting for a reply.

"I thought maybe I could help," I said as I lifted a sliver of turkey and ate it.

"Ha!" Anfesia said, "*Taakdaadax̂!*" The reference was to an Aleut story about a man who said he wasn't hungry but kept snacking whenever his hosts weren't watching.

After the kitchen was in order, Sophie thanked Anfesia, said good-bye to Mrs. Chagin and me, crossed herself, and went home. Mrs. Chagin and Anfesia poured themselves cups of tea and came to the table. Before Anfesia sat down, she went into her bedroom and brought out her weaving. She was finishing a very small basket, a thimble basket. We drank tea quite a long time. Anfesia wove. Agnes played solitaire. For once I didn't say anything. We had a good visit.

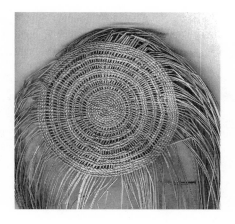

# 13

# Patterns

She weaves a stitch.
She lays a fine silk thread, tip down, along the next warp strand.
She weaves a stitch.
She pulls the long end of the thread, feels it slide beneath the stitch.
She pulls the long end of the thread until the short end almost disappears.
She almost pulls too far.
She wraps the thread around her weft two times.
She slides the thread beneath her left thumb to keep the tension firm.
She weaves a stitch.
The wrapped weft leaves a spot of color.
She weaves a stitch.
She weaves a stitch.
She carries the thread beneath the woven warp and brings it up.
She wraps the weft again two times.
She weaves a stitch.

With these spots of color, each the size of a single stitch, a design is built row by row much like cross-stitch work. Unlike cross-stitching, however, Aleut basketry stitches are not square and the vertical rows tend to slant slightly. Weavers who plot their designs on graph paper must always bear these facts in mind.

Although basketry has remained a cultural constant in Aleut life for thousands of years, there is today no vocabulary of traditional designs. A few patterns recorded by Jochelson around 1910 seem anomalies, for nowhere else are meanings ascribed to designs, and few of his explanations seem related to basketry. Because of this, while Aleut baskets may be seen as cultural artifacts, they must be viewed as independent objects of craft or art: classical shapes over which pure designs pass.

The basket is not a canvas, but stands defined by its own self: its shape and fiber, the evenness and fineness of its stitches. The designs, whatever their source, are expressions of individual weavers who may repeat favorite patterns, borrow designs from other weavers, and choose to use or not use the traditional placement of designs on the basket. The artist makes choices, and these selections shape the final work.

The best baskets are those whose designs cannot be read, or if derived from nature retain enough abstraction to remain perpetually fresh. Too much representationalism gets between the viewer and the basket, actually prevents the basket from being seen.

I incorporated green in many of my designs because it reminded me of summer.

"Didn't Aleuts have different colors beside green?" Anfesia complained one day. "Or is that your color? I notice you use it a lot like Sophie uses purple." She said her mother had used light colors for designs on covered bottles but darker colors on baskets.

Where did modern Aleut basketry designs come from? From cross-stitch books, from wallpaper, from magazines. There are a few baskets showing designs obviously derived from Aleutian natural history: ducks lifting into the air, majestic purple iris. But many baskets carry roses, garlands of roses, or medallions of pure geometry or stylized flowers.

One afternoon during the second or third year I was at Unalaska,

Anfesia was at the Center showing Addie Nordstrom one of her unfinished baskets. This basket was what she called her demonstration basket, which had been held by President Kennedy when he was a senator and had visited the Oregon centennial celebrations.

It was woven with very white grass with a crossed warp pattern on the bottom. The basket form was a cylindrical salt box. There was a fine string looped through the bottom of the basket at three points and brought together in the center where a single string was attached. She said this was used to hang the basket up while weaving on it as it was becoming too heavy to support in her hand. Her border design was a series of running purple diamonds each with a gold spot in the center. This was the design she said had started in 1842 and the origin of which she had challenged me to discover.

That morning I had received a package in the mail from my mother and was unwrapping it while Anfesia, Addie, and I sat at the table. Mom had sent some Kool Aid, two pairs of socks, and a box of Whitman's chocolates. Anfesia quietly wrapped her basket with a white handkerchief and placed it in a plastic bag. And then I saw it. There running around the chocolate box was the same design interrupted with the words "Started in 1842."

"Ha!" I exclaimed and shoved the box toward her.

"Doggone you!" she replied and hit the top of the box.

Aleuts continued to be elected to the city council and school board although the number of newcomers on those boards increased, and the balance of power shifted as people employed by the fish canneries established footholds in local government. Larry Shaishnikoff, Walter Dyakanoff, Anfesia, and others put in long hours as the school and city struggled to define themselves.

The city hired a manager and a full-time clerk. A public works department was established. King crab were bringing money into the town and the state was looking forward to extensive oil money.

The administrative position of head teacher had grown to that of a school principal. Before long the principal, Fred Kent, had persuaded the school board to name him superintendent of schools and he began making plans for a new building. Between 1970 and 1972, new teachers were hired who came to love the Aleutians and several would spend many years there: Al Dalrymple, Shelly Drake, Pat Eckhart, Mariana Foliart, Beverly Holmes, Jeff Jackman, Ben Kirker, Richard and Kay LaCourse, Sue Mershon, Jeff Randolph, and Coe Whittern. In 1972 a class of seven seniors graduated from high school, the first graduates since the four members of the class of 1951.

In many ways, however, Unalaska remained a small village. When the city manager complained about the slowness of the U.S. mail, our Father who worked at the post office stormed into his presence like the Holy Ghost of postal services. The city found itself hamstrung by a U.S. census that dramatically undercounted the residents. The enumerator had prepared the census from memory while sitting at home; perhaps it was a census of the people he thought ought to be living at Unalaska.

Phil was easing himself back to sobriety, and I was keeping him company while Anfesia attended a city council meeting. We were playing Scrabble, and it was one of those rare nights when I stood any chance of even approximating his winning score.

Anfesia came in laughing. The council had earlier hired another new cop and he had been at the meeting to make a request.

"You know they put up that speed sign by Verne's store," Anfesia said.

"Yeah," Phil said, "on the wrong side of the road."

When traffic came into town a 15-mile-limit sign stood on the left side of the road. Wooden water pipes ran somewhere on the right, and no one wanted to risk puncturing them with a metal post.

"The new cop wanted us to buy him a car," Anfesia said. He had asked the council how he was supposed to enforce the speed limit without a vehicle.

"Larry told him," Anfesia said as she tried to keep a serious expression, "he should run after the cars. If he couldn't catch them, they're speeding and he could mail them a ticket."

A Board of Health was established consisting of a city council member (Anfesia), the cannery nurse (Judy Fordham), the health aide (Platonida Gromoff), and a schoolteacher (myself). Before Anfesia and I had been appointed to the city's first Board of Health, we had served on an unofficial health council that tried to raise funds for health programs.

After the health board was formed we sent out a cry for help, a rather generalized cry with letters going to state and federal agencies as well as to the World Health Organization in Geneva. We didn't have the names of particular people to address, but soon the U.S. Public Health Service, through the Alaska Native Medical Center in Anchorage, came to our assistance. In December 1970 the Alaska Children's Services, with roots going back to the Jesse Lee Home that served the community from 1889 to 1924, sent Robert and Flora Fulton to assist in community development and planning regarding care of families and children. With them came their youngest son, Andy, whom Phil called Andyklootha.

A year later, through their assistance, a local nonprofit health and social service corporation was formed. We received invaluable support from Robert Fortuine, of the Alaska Native Medical Center, and from Lillie McGarvey on behalf of the Aleut League in Anchorage. Lillie, a daughter of Alice Hope, was renowned for her work in Indian health and she was an experienced and vocal administrator in Aleut regional organizations.

On the last day of 1971 Polly Lekanoff, Anna Shaishnikoff, Sophie Sherebernikoff, and I walked up to the rat-infested city hall and jail and signed incorporation papers for the Iliuliuk Family and Health Services. Pelagaia McCurdy had not been amused a few meetings before when I suggested we name the new organization the Unalaska Humane Society. The other members of the corporation were Pelagaia McCurdy, Shirley Shaishnikoff, Emil Berikoff, Jeanne Norton, and Robert Davis. Six members of the corporation were to be nominated by the local Aleut corporation and three by the city council, and we managed—for a year or two—to maintain the article in the bylaws stipulating that Aleut people constitute a majority of the board. The Fultons served as the first staff.

As a health board, and later as a health corporation, we were propelled by crises. The traumatic injuries that dangerous fisheries supplied, the ordinary cuts and illnesses of townspeople, the increased demands for services from canneries—all these made it easy to unite the community behind health services. The Elbow Room had a jar—at times, a bedpan—for donations for a new clinic and it was frequently filled. Canneries, fishing boats, individuals, the city itself—everyone contributed. But it was far more difficult to reach a consensus on how to serve the "family" part of "Family and Health Services." Factionalism within the community that erupted into virtual enmity tore at the corporation and nearly destroyed it. The Fultons were accredited by the state as social workers, and so while they remained at Unalaska, it was possible to place children in need with local families. They left in December 1972, however, and the community again found itself adrift.

An alcohol program had been started by Emil Berikoff prior to the formation of the health corporation, and it continued under the direction of Frank Poplawski, but only from year to year with the blessing of the state alcohol office. About as useful as an umbrella in Aleutian rain, mental health workers from Anchorage occasionally arrived—and always departed.

Anfesia held basketry classes in her home for beginning and experienced weavers. She had thought about establishing a club where only Aleut would be spoken and Aleut crafts practiced. She imagined it being held in the upstairs seaside room of the old Victorian Bishop's House that stood in stately disrepair near the church. The classes in her home were never large, but they included at least two young girls, Brenda Shelikoff and Okalena Lekanoff.

She was encouraged by the attention she received when she traveled as a representative of Aleut culture and spoke at the Alaska State Museum in Juneau, at the university in Fairbanks, and in Oakland, California, where she saw a beautiful basket made by Polly's grandmother. The early regional Aleut organizations invited her to speak at their meetings in Anchorage. She had been part of the Alaskan delegation at the Oregon centennial festivities, and loved to recount how then Senator John F. Kennedy had held her practice basket during his visit. She also told how while lecturing she had inadvertently rubbed the hair on a piece of fur against the grain causing the pelt to quiver and a woman standing in front of it to scream.

She felt a deep sense of accomplishment as a result of her basketry classes in Kodiak—not only because of the work of her students, especially Eunice Neseth, but also because of the weaving she was able to complete. From Kodiak she wrote that she was "weaving like I never wove before, trying to keep up with class. . . . I have finished ten napkin rings, 7 thimble baskets, four starters [beginning bottoms for new students] beside the class." She added, "It's so peaceful here. Weather is so good. Gentle sea breeze. Make you think of home. . . . They think I shouldn't go back [to Unalaska], but I feel my people need me. I have to go back."

After returning from one trip she wrote a short article for the local paper. While at the university she had translated Aleut and Russian and English. She had sung and chanted in Aleut and performed Aleut dances. "Our school will get a moving film on it and pictures 'cause it was for that purpose [that I went]. I tried very hard even if I was tired. I found out that they are interested in Aleut culture, but they have nothing on it. So teach your children to speak their Native language, even one word a day. You will help them if you do. Make them feel good and famous that they are Aleuts. Learn them the ways and how to do it if you know how. Start now. Don't wait til it is too late." She had ended with, "I am proud to be Aleut. Let your children feel the same."

I was always happy to have her back in Unalaska. Where else but in her home could I get such a sweet cup of tea? One afternoon she spooned some salmonberry jam into her cup and said, "The wife of a Russian priest used to drink her tea like this."

*Seal oil is prepared by cutting fat from the seal and placing it in an air-tight container. The fat will melt and the resultant oil may be poured*

*off. If kept in a cool place the oil will last indefinitely. The longer the oil
stands in the jar with the fat the more bitter it becomes. There is a
difference between fur seal and hair seal oil, but the novice cannot
detect it. The stomachs of the hair seal and the sea lion may be soaked,
scraped, blown, and used as containers for dried fish, or they may be
used as containers for making oil. They must be soaked before they can
be used as they will dry very stiff. The seal oil is rubbed over baidarkas
and on raincoats. Every so often these would be dried out and fresh oil
rubbed into them. Before the seal oil is used for this it must be prepared.
This oil is made by cooking the fat on the stove. The resultant oil is
burned slightly to prevent it from spoiling later on.*

*The intestine of a female sea lion will make one medium-length
raincoat. The skin of the sea lion is not used for water gear as it is not
waterproof. Before seal hide is used, it is boiled to a light brown to keep
it from smelling.*

Anfesia said that early Aleuts didn't count their design work
stitch-by-stitch and line-by-line. A weaver measured the harmony of
her basket by using her hand. The distance across the base was the
distance from the lower border to the top edge.

Occasionally in basketry but more often in gut sewing, colored
material was incorporated:

yellow: dry and slice the throat of the sculpin
red: during red tide boil sea eggs in urine
black: collect the long thin root that grows only along creek banks
white: dry the stomach of the sculpin on a board or use the
throats of seagulls that have been soaked, cleaned, and dried

*The Unalaska knob is begun in the regular fashion. Mrs. Shapsnikoff
wove a circle using a total of thirty-one warp strands. As no more warp
were added, the top began to curve. As it curved inward, she began to
skip warp (as the circumference grew smaller). These skipped warp
were dropped into the center. Using just a few remaining warp, a short
stem was woven and then she began weaving out again, gradually
picking up the dropped warp and eventually adding more for the top
of the cover.*

Using this technique of adding and dropping out warp, weavers covered bottles of various shapes. Sophie Pletnikoff employed this when she wove a cup and saucer and when she made small bell-shaped earrings. Augusta Dushkin used it masterfully when she wove around Japanese glass fishing floats that washed ashore on the sandy beach of Umnak. I used it when I wove Anfesia two small grass heads for dolls and when I wove a whale (into which a small Jonah carved by Phil was inserted).

> *Mats generally had only simple designs running across the work although she remembers seeing some made for the church that had triangles in them. The grass at Ruff's Bay is the whitest and strongest that she's seen here. After the first snow has gone is a good time to get grass. She showed me some bright magenta raffia, dating from her mother's time, and wondered how it had been dyed.*

Phil had once again obliterated me in a game of Scrabble. Now he stretched out on a rug before the stove in the living room and carved on a rattle. To get the small stones inside the carving he claimed he just took the pieces to church and prayed them in. Anfesia and I were weaving. I had turned the corner on a large basket, $3\frac{1}{4}$ inches in diameter, and had started the bottom border. She was at work on a pair of napkin rings for a friend in Kodiak.

By 1972, the king crab boom had receded, leaving only three crab processing plants still in operation. Smaller catches of crab, combined with a lack of housing, reliable water, and electricity had caused two other canneries to close up shop and the floating processors to find other ports. The city, however, had established enough of a base to begin providing services and making plans. Water was still supplied to the town and canneries through World War II sixteen-inch wood-stave pipes; most of it leaked out along the way. A garbage collection service was in place—if the garbage could be picked up before it blew away. A volunteer fire department had been established with sixteen members. The old diesel generators continued to supply the town with electricity—unless the attendant forgot to order fuel. The canneries supplied their own power through generators. The school enrollment had grown to a hundred and two. The city provided room for a small clinic in the back of the old military chapel; they had originally offered only the upstairs but soon realized the ill and injured would have a difficult time maneuvering the crooked, narrow steps. The front of this same chapel was converted into a gymnasium for the school and community. To make it more secular it was, as Phil said, emasculated; the steeple was cut off.

Of the ninety-six houses in town, a survey found forty-one to be poor and twenty to be below average; only five were listed as good. There was one telephone in town; people kept up on news by having a CB radio in every home. When telephones finally arrived, I heard Peter call Leonti on the CB, "Hello, Leonti, are you home? I'm going to call you on the phone. Over."

Phil was describing his recent stay in Anchorage. "Six meetings a week in addition to innumerable effing AA meetings all over Anchorage! I kept wishing I was a plain old drunk and could chuck those meetings. Even so I didn't have any desire to drink. Curious and fragile situation."

"You should take your brot to camp," Anfesia said to me.

"We'd both starve!" I laughed.

"Criminey!" Phil said.

Last summer his mother had spent two weeks at camp with his brother Tracy.

"It's good to be free," she said. "Go up and get blueberries for supper. Did you ever have them with fish livers? You should try it."

"*Taaĝux̂,*" Phil said.

"Well, I'm out of weavers [weft strands]," I said and began stretching the basket over a salt box. "This is excellent grass."

"It's from home," Anfesia said and meant Atka village.

"I gave Sophie some good Unalaska grass last week," I said as I wrapped the basket in a white handkerchief. "She seemed pleased with it."

"Damn girlfriends!" Anfesia smiled when she saw my reaction to her exclamation.

"I didn't show you what I bought from her, did I?" I knew I hadn't and I dreaded showing her Sophie's latest weaving.

"Criminey!" Phil said as I handed his mother a basket woven entirely out of plastic. Swiss straw was a commercial fiber that came in a world of bright colors. Sophie had woven with snow-white weft over snow-white warp. Once the sides were reached, she had alternated half-inch rows of white, red, and green. Fourteen bands of green and thirteen of red on a pure white background. The cover continued this same pattern up to a petite knob. Held within the confined classical shape, this Aleut basket sparkled like a sonata of Scarlatti.

"That Sophie!" Anfesia said. "Work, work, work."

I put the basket back in a paper sack and placed it in my pack with the basket I had been working on. I slipped on my coat and went to the door where Phil was shaking wood chips out of his carving towel.

The full spring moon had risen like an open boat, and Old Man Matfey wandered by heading down to the creek, drawn by some immeasurable tide. Phil and I stepped back inside. He put on his wool jacket and cap and explained to his mother where he was going. Matfey's monthly excursions into the creek had become more predictable as he aged. Phil would try to intercept him and bring him back to the house, where Anfesia would give him tea and bread. She went to the stove and moved the kettle over to the fire pot to bring it to a boil.

I said good night.

I walked out past the end of town and climbed a little above the cemetery. Moon shadows from crosses lined the gentle slopes. A startled ptarmigan, like the mountains, more white than brown, arced away, its gullet and wings scattering invisible guttural gravel. I stood awhile, the ground too wet for sitting. Except for lighted windows and streetlights the town was dark. The sharp peaks above Captain's Bay and the range of mountains north of Makushin Volcano rippled with reflected moonlight.

Back in town, at the corner where the isolated spruce trees stood, I heard a friend shouting at her lover. He had been drinking and refused to face her. If they saw me walking home, they were angry or drunk or gracious enough to continue. He whistled under the trees where the night was darker. She screamed at him. They were both young. Having seen this moon and heard these friends of mine, I went into the house, made fire, had tea and bread, and waited for sleep.

# 14

# An Altered Landscape

In the fall of 1970, Anfesia accompanied her friend Dorothy Jones back to Atka village, returning for the first time since she had left in 1905. Atka, some 350 miles west of Unalaska, was her father's village, the place her mother had moved to from Attu. It was where Anfesia had been born in 1900. The village was rebuilt following its burning by U.S. military forces during World War II, and consequently no buildings remained from Anfesia's childhood. She was so pleased that despite this she was able to locate where her house had stood. For her, Atka, however changed, was always home.

In Nikolski village on Umnak Island there is a house, roughly six feet square, with no windows or doors. Its four sides gather in a peaked roof. When Sergie Sovoroff was a boy (he was born in 1902) he defiantly hurled a spear at this building and within hours his arm began swelling. He endured five days of pain before the lanced arm healed. He once told me a visiting priest had taken an ax to the house, but before he could harm it he severely cut himself.

Of all structures in the Aleutian Islands, none is more mysterious than Nikolski's Monument House. It covers a remnant of the Aleutians' past, but Sergie did not know if it was good or evil. His father told him that no one actually knew what the house protected. That it had power, that it was to be preserved unmolested, was certain.

In June 1971, I visited Nikolski with my young *atcha* Jimmy Krukoff and his older brother, Sergie. We stayed a week visiting the boys' grandmother, Eva Chercasen. Jimmy and Sergie spent their days playing among the low hills, visiting the sheep ranch, riding a three-wheeler. Jimmy ended with his face decorated with bandages after he was thrown from the vehicle. I visited with local folks, skirted the two warring parties of anthropologists, and hiked the beach north of the village toward the White Alice site that dominated a distant cliff like an alien craft. I saw the Monument House, awash in young grass, just outside the fence of the churchyard. I crossed the low hills behind the village to the Pacific Ocean and walked to Sandy Beach, where a number of people had summer camps.

After I came back, Anfesia told me a little about her visit to Nikolski. I don't know if she went before or after her husband died on the coast of Umnak in the wreck of the *Umnak Native*, but while she was there someone died.

"The Nikolski people kept the real old ways," she said. "Longer than the Unalaska people."

Those who prepared the body for burial were not permitted to enter any home until they had cleansed themselves in a steambath. Anfesia remembered them having to take their meal in the hallway connecting the outside door with the living quarters.

Among the stories Anfesia heard was one that said the area had been visited by the Virgin Mary, the Theotokos, the Mother of God.

"When I went for a walk," her eyes twinkled at the confession, "I looked for her footprints which people said were around there."

Recent scholars have suggested the Monument House covers the remnants of a cross placed on the site of the first baptism in the Aleutians. In 1759 Stepan Glotov baptized a young Aleut boy, Mushkal', nephew of a prominent chief. A large cross was erected at the site. The boy was given the name Ivan Glotov and he began a distinguished career that led him to eventually become a Paramount Chief. Later Russians cut down this cross and used the lumber to build sleeping platforms in their barracks. As soon as they moved into the barracks, disease struck and over half of them died.

"Now, because of this," Veniaminov declared, "the Aleuts there do not dare to take even a chip of wood lying near the oratory." Certainly, the use of the word "oratory" and the awe in which it was held strongly suggest the Monument House. In 1806 Ivan Glotov built a chapel at Nikolski, the first in the Eastern Aleutians. According to Veniaminov, it was erected on the site of the cross.

The problem with identifying the Monument House with the cross is that the St. Nicholas Chapel was erected by Glotov on the south side of the local creek, whereas the Monument House is on the north side. Eventually the church was rebuilt on the north side of the creek, and the original site was again designated with a wooden cross.

In Bergsland's *Aleut Dictionary*, the word for Nikolski's Monument House is *ikax̂*, a word collected by the linguist Gordon Marsh in 1949 from Afinogen Ermeloff and Anton Bezezekoff. Marsh reported the house was also called "Adam's house" and "totem pole." The dictionary says the *ikax̂* is "a small house like a box with the stump of a pole in it—once a very high pole, destroyed by early Russians, with disastrous effect for them; the monument is supposed not to be damaged."

In 1938 the anthropologist William S. Laughlin, then a student with Aleš Hrdlička, heard from the Aleut priest Gregory Kochergin (born in St. Paul) that "This house marks and protects the stump of the tall pole that stood here when the first Russians arrived. It was so tall that a raven on top of it looked like a wren on the ground."

Sergie and Agnes Sovoroff were staying at their summer camp at Sandy Beach when I visited. Sergie took delight in recalling that when Agnes had written to me during my time in Vietnam, he had asked her to be sure to tell me to keep my head down. I had taken Sergie's class at Unalaska on making model baidarkas, and at Sandy Beach, Agnes gave me two small gut raincoats to dress the men in my model.

Although Sergie was somewhat reticent about the Monument House, he eventually made a tape recording in Aleut and sent it to Father Gromoff, who translated it. On the recording he said, "Even though I am gone they could mention my name concerning the old stories. Moreover, when I am gone if someone would mention my name in their prayers, I will thank you all very much."

Sergie heard the story of the *ikax̂* from his father who had received it from his grandmother. The pole had been so tall that on foggy days its top could not be seen. Briefly, a crew of stranded Russians tore it down to construct a shelter for themselves. Afterward they went to collect driftwood. Packing the wood was hard work—it usually had to be carried from the Pacific side of the island—and as each Russian stopped to rest, he died. One came to a small stream near the village and paused for a drink. As he bent over he fell in and drowned. He was a bearded man and the creek became known as Whisker Creek in Aleut.

The chapel constructed by Glotov was rebuilt numerous times. In 1886 it burned. In 1900 a new church was erected on the north side of the creek, at the far western end of the *ikax̂*. That year Sergie's father helped other villagers construct a house around the remnant of the pole, and it was his job to dig post holes for the corners using a bone-digging stick. He dug each hole to an arm's depth, and at the bottom of one of the holes he felt boards. In 1930 the house was replaced with a new structure. At this time the remnant of the pole was about a foot tall. Later when repairs needed to be made, Sergie asked Dorofey Chercasen and Val Dushkin to make them. They were reluctant to touch the Monument House until Sergie assured them they would be fine because he had asked them to do this project.

The disparity between Veniaminov's account and village accounts about the Monument House is notable because of the accuracy of many Aleut oral traditions. Nikolski people passed down the story of the 1764 Aleut/Russian conflict with a remarkable accuracy that was confirmed by archaeological excavations. No excavation can explain the metamorphosis of the cross into a tree or the ancient tree into a Christian symbol.

Anfesia had been to the Monument House during her stay at Nikolski. "I looked through a crack in the wall," she recalled, "and saw the trunk leaning at an angle." Unfortunately, her account differs radically from Sergie's and must be considered less accurate. It is, however, of interest precisely because it was her version. She said she heard the story from a member of the Bezezekoff family whose traditional home had been a village somewhere in the Islands of the Four Mountains.

When people arrived at Nikolski, she said, they found the tree. It was very tall and lost in the clouds. God somehow communicated with the Aleuts through it. "I always thought some holy person came down it," she said. The tree was cut down at night. She didn't know whether local people, Russians, or Americans had felled it, but in the morning people found it lying across the church like a mother embracing her child. The Nikolski people then buried the trunk and built a protective house over the stump. Something—but she couldn't remember what—happened to the ground where the tree was buried.

Finally, one further note on the Monument House. One afternoon at Unalaska, Sergie Sovoroff and Father Gromoff were talking while I sat with them. Sergie said that when people first came to Umnak, to Nikolski, and saw the pole it was very tall and twisted like rope (*umna-x̂*) or kelp (*umya-x̂*). The island's name derived from that observation.

Agnes Sovoroff was working on a small basket at Sandy Beach. Jenny Krukoff, the great Attu weaver, had died of illness and exposure outside her house on November 6, 1969. She was the last survivor of seven Attu women who had spent a year cutting, curing, and splitting grass with which they wove a number of fine baskets. These were traded at Unalaska for lumber and materials with which the Attu people constructed a new church in 1932. Jenny had been Nikolski's primary weaver and only after her death did younger women begin to make baskets for sale. Before long Agnes Sovoroff, Augusta Dushkin, and Christine Dushkin had acquired reputations as fine weavers. All three women made occasional trips to Unalaska and would occasionally have baskets for sale at one of the local stores.

When Agnes told me how she had learned to weave with Jenny as her teacher I was immediately reminded of my first lesson with Sophie Pletnikoff. Agnes said Jenny would take her work, look at it closely, and toss it to her with the comment, "That's not the way it's done." Agnes would try again and again with the same results. She began to get angry with the older woman.

"If she would have handed it to me nicely I wouldn't have minded, but she just tossed it! Finally," Agnes said, "one time she looked at it and said, 'That is how you do it,' and she sort of smiled. Then I lost my anger."

Like the pinnacle rock near Agamgik Bay in Beaver Inlet that Veniaminov identified with a petrified demon of Aleut legend, the Monument House of Nikolski remains a mystery. It is rooted in a distant past that may seem to have little connection with contemporary Aleut life. Yet within Aleut communities, through cycles of grass, across the growth and decay of seasons, decade by decade, lines of continuity extend back to that time before Europeans arrived. The following example is from Anfesia's family, but each family has its own traditions. Unfortunately, the names of few women have survived in historical records. That they were primary teachers, however, cannot be doubted: Witness Anfesia herself and Sergie Sovoroff's great-grandmother, who conveyed the story of the *ikax̂* to Sergie's father. Anfesia knew and learned much from Chief Alexei Yatchmenef (1866-1937) of Unalaska and from weavers Mary Prokopeuff Levigne (1876-1919) and Maggie Prokopeuff (1857-1938) of Attu. They in turn had received instruction from a generation that included the storyteller Cedor Solovyov (1849-1912) and the Aleut priest Nicholas Rysev (1828-1910) of Unalaska and these two had known the Aleut priests Innokentii Shaishnikoff (1824-1883) and Lavrentii Salamatov (1818-1864), who had been students of Iakov Netsvetov (c. 1804-1864).

Netsvetov, the first Aleut priest, had known the great chief of Amlia in the 1830s, Nikolai Dediukhin, and he was acquainted with Ivan Pan'kov, the Aleut chief and linguist who assisted Veniaminov. Netsvetov was at Unalaska in 1807 when Hieromonk Gideon visited and chrismated both the young Iakov and the elderly Ivan Glotov, the builder of the chapel at Nikolski, the first Aleut to receive baptism in the Eastern Aleutians. Glotov in turn had known the earliest Russians to enter waters in the Eastern Aleutians—Stepan Glotov and Ivan Solov'ev. He had known those leaders who sought to coexist with the Russians and he had known defiant warriors like Itchadaq and Inglagusaq of Unalaska, who had defeated the Russians in the mid-1760s but who gave their lives in later battles. But did Ivan Glotov or Itchadaq or Inglagusaq know about the petrified demon in Beaver Inlet or have knowledge about whatever is in the Monument House at Nikolski? If it had been a cross then Glotov knew of its erection, its destruction, the preservation of its base. Glotov, too, would have heard of the destruction of a tree or pole by Russians even if he had been absent with other Russians when the tree was felled, even if he (confidant of many Russians) had not been privy to knowledge lost with people like Itchadak (in whose eyes Ivan Glotov must have seemed a traitor).

Whatever traditions were lost across two centuries, whatever new customs developed, weaving remained a perpetual reminder of the weaver's place in the order of the world. In harvesting grass, the weaver bowed to the earth. In preparing grass, the weaver praised sun and rain.

For me, persistent outsider, weaving had changed the way I saw the island. No longer were the long blades of grass only a sweet excess of nature. They were now fiber, warp and weft. Weaving illumined the specifics of that place, its history and culture, the way light at dusk wraps the leaves until they glow from within, as though they had swallowed light. Any craft tied to the land will do this: carding wool, mixing the clay, feeding the fire in the wood kiln, knowing the leaf that fed the wood that sits now planed and waiting for the knife. Or if you are like Phil Tutiakoff, knowing from the sea-washed bark of driftwood, the beach-rasped naked log, the elasticity, strength, and texture of the wood.

Weaving was anarchy's nemesis, creating order from seemingly random materials, providing a physical continuity from season to season during times of village turmoil.

Like the elusive footprints of the Theotokos at Nikolski, like the stories surrounding the Monument House, each basket carries traces from the Aleutians' past. The finest baskets rise to perpetual celebration. So dance and stories, the bentwood bowl and hat, stone, ivory and grass, applaud master artists who risk all to capture in an object or performance a transforming moment. In some of the poems of Theodore Roethke there is a pure delight in being, and to this can be added, if I read certain of his poems correctly, an emptiness, an openness, a staying up all night to see the land we love. Combined, these states of mind go far to make not an illumined life, nothing so grand, but something akin to that elusive moment William Blake admonished us to seize:

> *There is a Moment in each Day that Satan cannot find,*
> *Nor can his Watch Fiends find it; but the Industrious find*
> *This Moment & it multiply, & when it once is found*
> *It renovates every Moment of the Day if rightly placed.*

This, it seems to me, is what the finest baskets do.

After Sergie, Jimmy, and I returned to Unalaska, Jimmy and I flew to Anchorage. His parents had given him permission to spend the summer in Missoula, Montana, where my sister lived and where I would be attending summer school. My parents drove to Anchorage, where Jimmy and I joined them. Before starting back along the Alcan highway, however, we met Anfesia and enjoyed her company for a day at Portage Glacier. At Missoula I worked on a long paper on Aleut basketry which Anfesia corrected once Jimmy and I were back at Unalaska.

I began making marathon day hikes along Beaver Inlet. I would stride out from town to Humpy Cove and take the gradual rise through the low pass to Beaver Inlet. From Agamgik to Chaluuknax̂ to the outskirts of Ugadaga I would try to stay slightly inland to avoid the difficult walking along the beach. Usually late afternoon or evening had arrived by the time I descended the road to the head of the valley. It was an exhausting hike, but when it was completed I felt I had surrounded the island in a long embrace. It was, however, an embrace few wanted to share. I persuaded Rick and Kay LaCourse on one occasion and Shelly Drake (with Ruth and Tom Nighswander visiting from Anchorage) on another to make the hike with me.

As tired as death, only gravity dragging us down the mountain road into town, they never forgave me.

In March 1972 Anfesia attended the Arctic Winter Games in Whitehorse, Canada, to participate in a demonstration of Native crafts. She had been debating whether or not to go, and one day she said, "I think I need to leave here for awhile anyway."

Phil was carving a sugar spoon from scrub alder and looked up. His mother said, "People want Aleut things, but no one will do them."

"Except Sophie," Phil said and smiled.

"Except *Tunuxtaada*," Anfesia agreed. "These Aleuts are like wheelbarrows. They never move unless we push them."

"Criminey!" Phil said.

"But I'm sure we'll make out somehow," she added. She went to Whitehorse and took along the small fish basket I had made under her instruction.

One morning while she was gone, I stopped by Mrs. Moller's house. My hopes rose when I smelled freshly baked bread, and sure enough she served me tea and fried bread. We talked about Anfesia.

"The only time I miss her," Mrs. Moller said, "is when I eat fresh fish and when I go to church."

Never was there a more appropriate pairing: fresh fish and church. Place and belief united by craft. A cross, a tree, a house guarding a sacred spot. All things made by hand in ordered exultation confirm the weaver's ordinary craft.

Generations of hands touching each other, curled like blades of grass around a growing stem, open and here, on Sophie's plastic checkered tablecloth, on Anfesia's plywood kitchen counter crowded with fish and tea, a jubilation of baskets.

From Nikolski village to Sandy Beach, the path across the low hills gradually climbed to a crest. If the day had been clear, I could have gazed to my left onto the enormous rim of the Pacific Ocean and, to my right, faced the vast plains of the Bering Sea. My vision blocked by the world's curve, I could have seen with my mind's eye water beyond that watery horizon. During my visit, however, the view was cut short by fog. There on Umnak Island that early summer afternoon I could only imagine what a small chunk of earth this land mass was in all that water of the western world. Unencumbered by ecstasy, I crouched down out of the wind.

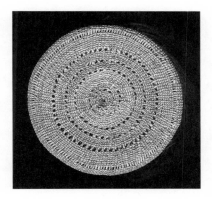

## 15
# The Finished Basket

In early morning moments I have mapped impossible hikes into bays in Beaver Inlet I have yet to visit. I imagine a trek to Tanaskan Bay and up the mountain to the soapstone deposit, where I chip out a beautiful block and carry it back to Mrs. Hope's daughter, that excellent sculptor Gert Svarny. I see myself farther along the shore searching for the spot where whale hunters attached a grass rope that spanned the width of the inlet. New configurations of familiar plants, light altered by unexplored cliffs and shoulders of descending mountains bring me finally to a point on Amugul Bay, where water from the Pacific Ocean surges past.

How is it this is never home, this place where the heart is so at rest? This place which now I could never leave however far I traveled, however long I was gone. Here where wind wove grass into natural baskets, where cold and rain pressed it into white mats covering a winter beach.

My desire to visit the bays of Beaver Inlet had a nineteenth-century romantic taint, an excursion into wilderness. It was the same attitude that took me outside the barracks at Fort Leonard Wood, Missouri, one summer night in 1969. The manned spacecraft was scheduled to arrive on the moon in a few hours and I wanted to see it one last time unsullied.

Who makes decisions? Who calls a place home?

Anfesia's constant warning on two fronts: Preserve your traditions and get yourself into positions where you can make decisions.

> *Since almost everyone is interested in Aleut things and values them, Aleut children should be taught their language and the ways of the ancestors so they can be carried on. Things I heard of long ago are happening. Unknown people are coming, taking over our land and the things we made our living with. So let's get together and prevent these by speaking up. We have no head man, no one to go to when we need help. So let us find someone to be our Chief. At that time we could talk over problems, and what was decided he could instruct us to do. Whenever there is suggestions for what could be done to make our community better, if you know any, don't be afraid to say it. . . . so whoever wants to learn is welcome to join.*

Matching deeds to words was not simple. When Anfesia asked me who I thought should be chief, I named a local Aleut whom I greatly respected. She scoffed, "He's not even an Aleut!" I said, "But he's got a great sense of humor."

If I had learned anything, that was part of it.

> *Finishing the basket. When weaving has been completed, the warp strands must be secured in a finishing stitch. When you are ready to finish a basket, you will be in a weaving position, having just twined warp A. The next warp will be warp B. The weft on the bottom is weft D and the one on top is weft C. Take warp A and bring it up over weft D and warp B. Twist it firmly and place it behind weft C so that it lays*

*along the line of weaving and can be held in place by the thumb and fingers of the left hand. Now twine a stitch using weft C and weft D.*

*This stitch has twined over warp B and left warp A up on top. Warp A is now brought down and tucked under the basket. To do this bring it in front of the top weft (D), down under the basket and pull it far to the left. You may feel it "snap" into a locked position. You are now ready to follow the same procedure in securing warp B.*

*When the last warp has been secured you will be left with one warp and two weft strands. The rest of the warp will be tucked up inside the basket. Thread the longest warp on a needle. Cut the remaining warp and weft off about ⅛ to ¼ of an inch and press these short ends against the basket rim. Using the threaded weft, stitch over these two short pieces several times. The last stitch is taken back through the looped stitches and the weft is cut off.*

*The warp that are tucked up inside the basket may now be cut off. Cut them off to about ½ an inch, perhaps a little more. Place the basket back on its form and twist it so as to straighten the weaving. Cover the basket sides with a piece of heavy paper and wrap some cloth around it, tying it securely in place. Let the basket sit wrapped for some time until the warp are set in this tucked position. They may then be clipped off much shorter.*

I took the year 1972-1973 off from teaching in order to complete courses for my teaching certification and to work on a master's degree at the University of Alaska in Fairbanks. In November Anfesia stayed with me in my little apartment while she made recordings in Aleut and English for the university. She examined transcriptions of the folktales Jochelson had collected in 1909 and 1910 that Michael Krauss of the Alaska Native Language Center had secured from the New York Public Library and from Gordon Marsh, who had worked on the material in the late 1940s. Anfesia was especially pleased when she read a narrative written by Chief Alexei Yatchmenef. She began studying the new Aleut orthography designed in 1972 which was replacing that developed from a Cyrillic script in the nineteenth century. One evening she said, "Here I am over seventy years old and learning how to read all over again. Never say you're too old to learn!"

She returned home and on December 16 she wrote that Tracy and Phil were both in town: "Times are like long time ago all together." Vincent, her grandson, was preparing a room in the house for his wife and expected child who were due back from Anchorage soon. Doretta was one of Nick and Polly Lekanoff's daughters. The child, a son named Vincent Michael, Jr., would be born the end of December. There had been lots of geese and twice they had eaten geese for supper. The temperature had dropped to twelve degrees above zero, unusually cold for the Aleutians. Her water had frozen but a westerly wind had made the sea "real nice," and I remembered whitecapped waves breaking above silver gray swells. She wrote that Addie Nordstrom "is so much in my mind since I came back."

In early January a letter came that she had written on December 22. Phil had taken her out to a Russian fishing vessel to translate for the nurse, who had been called to treat a sick seaman. Anfesia wrote that she had kept talking so as not to cry over the young man. She got angry at the Russians and swore at them.

By January 1973 she had been growing weaker for some time, and Vince told me the boys had asked her to take it easy and not work so hard. When she insisted on helping to clean and paint the Sergie Chapel for Russian Christmas on January 7, Phil told her that if she had to come to the church, she was not to do anything. She could supervise. Nevertheless, she wanted to make sandwiches and tea for the workers, and so she did.

Vince had wondered why his Gram had insisted on baptizing his and Doretta's son before the priest returned to town. The Gromoffs had moved to Old Harbor on Kodiak Island, and Father Fryntsko, the authoritarian priest at Unalaska, was making a prolonged visit at Atka during November and December. Anfesia was too weak to lift the baby three times as was normally done but she conducted the baptism in her home. This undoubtedly afforded her great satisfaction as she had become very fond of her great-grandson. Vince was perhaps dearer to her than any of her sons. She loved them all in different ways, but Vince was always the youngest, the little boy, and so his son meant very much. Flora Fulton said Anfesia had babysat the young-ster so that Doretta and Vincent could go to the movies together.

During the Christmas service she read in Aleut, Phil read in Russian, and Vince read in English. Flora told me it was an especially beautiful service. Because of the priest's absence, Anfesia was able to have her own way regarding church services. This undoubtedly pleased her greatly, as she was often in disagreement with the manner in which he carried out the services. He arrived at the airport on Monday, January 15, as Anfesia was being carried aboard the plane. Her illness had become critical.

Anfesia's condition had been aggravated by her failure to rest thoroughly. Cora Gray, the nurse, told me Anfesia's lungs were filling with fluid and putting pressure on her heart. According to Phil, the abnormalities of her chest cavity, as a result of tuberculosis of the spine, complicated the situation. On Saturday the 13th Cora had ordered her to stay in bed and give her heart a rest. Phil was visiting Peter and Laresa Dushkin on Dutch, and when Cora called him he came over and stayed with his mother constantly. The festivities of Christmas and New Year, interspersed by days of caroling with the colorful rotating stars, were always stressful times, and when people realized the seriousness of her condition they gave her quiet to rest.

Tracy, her son, "old man," said he came home from work at noon on Monday the 15th as Anfesia was leaving for the hospital. She walked to the stretcher. He never liked to say good-bye, so he greeted her and left the house.

Once Anfesia was aboard the YS-11 and the stretcher placed at the back, opposite the door, Phil asked Father Fryntsko if he had his portable communion kit. He said he did and Phil asked him to see his mother. The priest began talking with Anfesia until the plane was about to leave. Phil bent over and could tell his mother had not received the sacrament. He raised his voice to the stewardess and announced, "Father is going to say a prayer now!" The priest jumped up and only then began the sacrament.

Later Father Fryntsko said Anfesia had told him she would not be coming back. He had insisted that she would get well and again be with them before long.

Sandra Moller, Alice Moller's granddaughter, was returning to Fairbanks, where she was a freshman at the university. Without her glasses on, Anfesia didn't recognize her until she came up to say hello. Also on the plane was Hughie McGlashan, who had fractured his collar bone in a high school basketball game the night before.

Phil said his mother initially wanted to sit up. Between Cape Sarichef and Cold Bay, she had some tea. After the plane landed in Cold Bay, Melody, the stewardess, said either she or Phil should remain on board during the brief layover. Phil stayed. The plane was not long on the ground and after taking off, it continued to fly very low. The pilots were helpful; Phil reported they skimmed about seventeen minutes off the flight time. The pilot and copilot made several trips back to see how she was.

Shortly out of Cold Bay, Anfesia asked for a sleeping pill. She began to fail rapidly. Phil and Melody tried using oxygen but it only inflated her lungs. Then Phil began mouth-to-mouth resuscitation after asking if anyone else knew how. George Gray and his son Alan assisted him. After Phil got the rhythm established, five Air Force men stood, took off their coats, and joined the line. They did not allow Phil back in the line but continued their efforts for over two hours until reaching Anchorage.

A Catholic chaplain out of Cold Bay offered to administer the last rites after the resuscitation had started and Phil gave permission. A traveling evangelist also was aboard and asked if he could pray. Again Phil gave the okay, and later remarked how several passengers glanced uneasily as the evangelist leaned forward and prayed with emphasis. Phil, however, said he appreciated the minister's efforts and concern.

The crew had called ahead for an ambulance and doctor; however, upon landing they learned that neither had arrived. A Reeve employee was sent for a resuscitator from the airport fire department, but no one on the plane knew how to operate it. Phil had been unable to detect a pulse in her wrist and instead had observed an artery in her neck. Now even that stopped. There were no vital signs. He gave permission for her body to be covered.

Phil had telegrammed me in Fairbanks at ten that morning: "Am taking mom to ANS Hospital today very sick please pray for her acknowledge by mail soonest will keep in touch." Before I received the message Lillie McGarvey had called from Anchorage to tell me Anfesia had died. I arranged to fly home with Phil and his mother's body.

When word reached Unalaska of Anfesia's death, her family and friends were stunned. There was snow on the ground. The wind blew. Close to midnight Sophie Sherebernikoff went to her back porch to sweep away the snow from the door. As she stood there with the broom, she heard the rumbling approach of an earthquake. Suddenly several strong jolts shook the town. A number of people recalled how they had stood up in alarm. Vince, overwhelmed with sorrow, was struck with panic for a moment and immediately thought of his gram.

*Sanakux̂!* Enough!

Flora reminded me about a dream Anfesia had related the previous summer. She dreamed she had died but somehow stayed around to watch the proceedings. She had told the boys not to make any fuss over her—and they certainly weren't! They wrapped her up in an old canvas and dragged her over to the corner of the lot near Bill Berikoff's fence, where they plopped her into a shallow hole! She had stood around watching this and was indignant. "I told them not to make a fuss over me, but I didn't expect them to just wrap me in an old dirty canvas! They weren't even nice!"

She was amused by the whole dream.

She told me once that she didn't need to be taken to the church for services. Neither of her husbands had been taken there, and so there was no reason for her going there. She could be buried near her mother's grave where she had planted a fir tree. But when the end did come, her family selected the most excellent location and all proceedings carried the deepest affection. Her grandson Vince selected the grave site, choosing a spot next to the bell tower on the bay side, beside Alexei Yatchmenef and with room for the memorial marker for his grandfather who had died in the wreck of the *Umnak Native*.

Vince met Phil and me at the airport. Greg, Greg Jr., Tracy, and others were waiting at the creek in town when Phil, Vince, and I arrived with the coffin in Mac McDonald's new ferry. The coffin was placed on the back of a pickup for the ride up to the house. We carried it through the back door where Greg's wife Marina, Dora Kudrin, her daughter Polly Lekanoff, and Polly's daughter Doretta Tutiakoff, and others were waiting. The coffin was placed on two chairs in the living room in the corner where the icons hung.

It was a wooden coffin covered with gray flannel. After opening the top half, women placed paper flowers on the closed half and began arranging the interior with decorative lace. A small semicircle of blue forget-me-nots was placed around her head. This remained until Dora Kudrin and Mariah Lekanoff decided the simple plastic flowers were not colorful enough. They unwound an orange crepe flower Arlene Moses had made and wrapped a piece of orange crepe around each blue flower. While they worked, they spoke and joked to Anfesia. When Anfesia's pal, Agnes Chagin, came and stood by the body of her dear friend, it sounded like they were again sitting having tea while Agnes scolded her: "Why did you do this to me, Pal? You shouldn't have done this to me."

Vince wanted some other clothing placed on his gram as she was wearing her old quilted, dark blue, windbreaker jacket. The older women said that couldn't be done.

All the mirrors were covered according to custom. Shortly the priest arrived and conducted a short service. That evening a second service was held. Afterward Phil, commenting on the priest's remarks, wondered how his mom would have liked being compared to a basketball team. We all laughed over that.

All through Wednesday, friends continued visiting the house. The Orthodox would cross themselves as they entered. When Dora came once she knocked and Myria scolded her. This was not done while the body remained in the house. All that evening and night friends were in the kitchen drinking tea and talking quietly. Shirley Fredericks and Ruth Shaishnikoff were of great comfort as they quietly kept the kitchen cleaned up after all the guests. Other friends were in the living room with Anfesia. To the left of the head of the coffin someone always stood and read from the Psalms, either in English or Russian. Above her head a holy lamp burned slowly before the icon of St. Nicholas. When someone came in from the cold, he or she would stand awhile by the oil heater at the back of the room to get warm.

On Wednesday evening Phil cut out squares of white paper and drew the Cyrillic letters for the Orthodox phrase that would circle the upper sides of the coffin. Three high school students, Leonard Lekanoff, Bill Shaishnikoff, and Okalena Lekanoff, joined me as we helped cut the letters as Phil drew them. We moved the project upstairs, where Phil joked that he had made this particular verse many times and it was always different! When the letters were ready, he took pins and a string and made a straight guideline a few inches below the top of the coffin. He and Polly Lekanoff closed the lid of the coffin and arranged the letters around its circumference prior to gluing them onto the sides. When all was finished, the top half of the coffin was again opened and the string and pins, never to be used again, were tucked into the closed half, out of view.

Nick Lekanoff stayed late at the house keeping his wife and Tracy company during the long hours of reading. I asked Phil if it would be acceptable if I took a turn reading from the Psalms. He said, yes, certainly. He asked me if he could put two small plastic plates imbedded with flowers from the Holy Land into the coffin. I had given these to Anfesia after my visit to Israel. I told Phil I had brought a packet and would put it in the coffin if he approved. And so I placed a finely woven Chinese envelope beside her containing rose petals from Bahji, a shard of blue glass from Bahá'u'lláh's birthplace, carnation petals from the garden of Ridvan—one white and one red—a stone from Mount Carmel, a shell from the seawall where the Mediterranean strikes the Holy Land at Akka. When I had finished reading from Psalm 119, Nick and Polly's son Leonard began his turn. I left long before Nick went home.

I was told that Sophie Pletnikoff came to the house briefly. She herself was in failing health, but she had walked from New Town to pay her respects.

Grief went deepest for the members of Anfesia's family. Each sat alone; each stood or walked alone. They leaned on one another, spoke gently, laughed quietly. They knew how much Anfesia had meant to many of us. They were gracious beyond compassion and made us welcome. We tried to keep talking, but every so often there were long breaths of silence. Grief lay like open water. On its great shore we kept each other company, huddled together, solitary and frightened.

About ten the next morning, I was sitting on the couch near the coffin when the sun broke through the clouds, came through the front porch windows and into the living room. For a few moments the sunlight shone across the paper flowers resting on the coffin, releasing their brilliant colors.

When we followed her to church that afternoon, it was calm and cold. A slight breeze came out of the northern sky. The clouds opened to patches of blue. We went out the back door of her house to the side road. As we passed beside the trees at the corner I saw the cold sea beyond. Then the procession bearing her closed coffin turned left and continued up the street. Mrs. McCurdy was returning from the church and dashed into her house until the coffin entered the yard and then she joined the procession. Bells tolled as the coffin passed under them through the narthex and into the nave.

Then the Service for the Dead began, prescribed, melodious, and final. Near its conclusion, I sensed the depth of her absence. Alone in the company of my friends, in the rigorous splendor of the candlelit church, without hesitancy or volition, in a wave of supplication, I was brought to my knees.

When the service was over, Phil, Tracy, Greg, Vince, Greg, Jr., and Peter Walter Stepetin carried the coffin out through the double doors. The grave site was on their immediate right, but they turned left to circumambulate the church. It was cold and slippery, and Dora Kudrin took my arm with a stiff, arthritic hand. As the procession passed the back of the church behind the altar, a breeze off the bay struck us. Spots of blue appeared in the sky. The steep lawn on the bay side was icy, so the coffin had to be taken down and around all the other graves. Dora must have thought Anfesia was going to be buried at the bottom of the hill because she began to protest when she saw the coffin carried down the slope. "Not down there!" she said, and we hurried forward.

*Sanakux̂.*

*Sanakux̂.*

So this was it. This is how to weave a basket. This is how I learned to weave a basket. Craft and place merged into a single landscape: an island of sea cliffs and conflicts, of pain, desires, and exaltation, an island between sea and ocean where small blossoms anchored in openness.

After Anfesia's death, I returned to Unalaska. I came back not to carry on her work—her work was finished—but to do the job she had given me, to be one of an increasing number of voices speaking for Aleut culture. While other voices grew silent, younger Aleuts became proponents of dance and storytelling; practitioners of weaving, painting, sculpture, and bentwood crafts; students of language, poets. Just as Kamgiligan, the Spirit of Makushin Volcano, had become an Aleut himself, so Aleuts continued to transform themselves, continuously striving to improve their lives, but always inexplicably retaining a core of identity as Aleut.

After his mother's death, through the sheer magnitude of his intellect, the breadth of knowledge and experience he could summon into conversations, Phil Tutiakoff became chairman of the regional nonprofit corporation. In the years immediately before his own death in 1985, he would be integral to the quest for righting the injustices Aleuts had suffered during World War II. With the support of his wife, Flora, he would devote himself completely to this task. His letters from that time—private and as "chairman of the board"—comprise a stunning testimony to the intellectual and moral vigor of the Aleut people.

Phil repeatedly called Aleuts "the best people on earth," deliberately countering decades of poisonous stereotyping. Part of what he meant, I thought, was their absolute integration with a particular place. The weaving together of people, place, crafts, and language creates an ethnic landscape anchoring human choices, opening possibilities for goodness unimagined by outsiders. This is what I learned to teach. I thank those who taught me.

One night on the white, sandy beach at Cam Ranh Bay, in a blaze of political naiveté, I had written, "New earth, new ocean, but the same embracing sky and moon." But this was true. The children of my students have picked the stalks of wild rye in the midst of a community altered beyond imagining from what it was when I first arrived. This woven memoir is for them. They may find it instructive. The world is still in flux. Some of these circumstances may come again. People should be so lucky.

# References and Notes

Whenever possible, spelling of Aleut words has been standardized with Knut Bergsland's *Aleut Dictionary: Unangam Tunudgusii*, Alaska Native Language Center, University of Alaska Fairbanks, 1994.

1. AN AUTUMN HIKE
"No other area in the world is recognized as having worse weather...."
—*United States Coast Pilot 9: Pacific and Arctic Coasts*, 7th edition, United States Government Printing Office, Washington, D.C., 1964: 165. "Glacier with tongues"—*Geology of Unalaska Island and Adjacent Insular Shelf, Aleutian Islands, Alaska*, Harald Drewes, et al., Geological Survey Bulletin 1028-S, United States Government Printing Office, Washington, D.C., 1961: 587. The story about Kamgiligan—"Kamgiligan - Future Head" told by Isidor Solovyov in *Aleut Tales and Narratives*, edited by Knut Bergsland and Moses L. Dirks, Alaska Native Language Center, University of Alaska Fairbanks, 1990: 156-161. Von Langsdoroff's account of his hike from Ugadaga Bay is from *A Voyage Around the World, 1803-1807*, translated and annotated by Victoria Joan Moessner, The Limestone Press, Fairbanks, Alaska, 1993: 10-11. For the name Nawan-Alaxsxa, see Knut Bergland's *Aleut Dictionary*, 1994: 283. Veniaminov's June 12, 1827, trek is found in *Journals of the Priest Ioann Veniaminov in Alaska, 1823 to 1836*,

translated by Jerome Kisslinger, University of Alaska Press, 1993: 55-56. The 1869 statement from Aleuts in San Francisco was printed in the San Francisco newspaper *Daily Alta California*, February 27, 1869: 1.

2. VILLAGE LIVES, VILLAGE ELDERS
Information on the history, structural, and religious significance of the Church of the Holy Ascension may be found in publications by Barbara Sweetland Smith and Lydia T. Black. Henry Swanson's story of the drunken bumblebees is found in *The Unknown Islands: Life and Tales of Henry Swanson*, Cuttlefish VI, Unalaska City School District, Unalaska, Alaska, 1982: 203-204.

4. A SUMMER HIKE
Aleutian plant associations were described in Eric Hulten's *Flora of the Aleutian Islands*, Second Edition, published by J. Cramer, Weinheim, Germany; New York, N.Y., 1960: 38-44.

5. VILLAGE LIVES, VILLAGE LAUGHTER
Except for one, all of the stories from Henry Swanson are more or less taken from *The Unknown Islands*. The versions in that book were often assembled from several tellings of the same story. In 1995, the small, covered bottle made by Molly Lukanin was donated to the Ounalashka Corporation by my aunt Annie Wake

to whom I had given it. Veniaminov on "nomadic Aleuts" is found in *Journals of the Priest Ioann Veniaminov in Alaska, 1823 to 1836*: 176, 184.

6. A BEGINNER'S BASKET
Information on Aleut basketry may be found in several publications: "Aleut Basketry," Anfesia T. Shapsnikoff and Raymond L. Hudson, *Anthropological Papers of the University of Alaska*, 1974, 16-2:41-69. "Designs in Aleut Basketry," Raymond L. Hudson, *Faces, Voices & Dreams*, Division of Alaska State Museums and the Friends of the Alaska State Museum, 1987: 63-92. *Aleut Basket Weaving*, Kathy Lynch (with Sophie Pletnikoff), Adult Literacy Laboratory, Anchorage Community College, 1974. *How To Attu: A Guide to Making Your Own Attu Basket*, Virginia Samuelson and Eunice Neseth, Arctic How To Books, Kodiak, Alaska, 1981. Jenny Krukoff's mother's song was sung by Anfesia Shapsnikoff on a recording made by Dorothy M. Jones in Cold Bay, Alaska, sometime in the 1960s.

7. APPROACHING SMALL BAY
For information on Aleut plant names and uses, see *Unugulux Tunusangin, Oldtime Stories*, Unalaska City School District, Unalaska, Alaska. Names of individual plants may also be consulted in Bergsland's *Aleut Dictionary*.

8. A WINTER HIKE
"It is quite clear that the mosaic of plant communities . . ."—*Flora of the Aleutian Islands*, Eric Hulten: 40-41. Veniaminov on weather patterns is found in *Notes on the Islands of the Unalashka District*, Ivan Veniaminov, translated by Lydia T. Black and R.H. Geoghegan, The Elmer E. Rasmuson Library Translation Program, University of Alaska Fairbanks, and

The Limestone Press, Kingston, Ontario, Canada, 1984: 47-55. Henry Swanson on being a weather prophet: *The Unknown Islands*: vi. Veniaminov on the March 17, 1833, storm: *Notes on the Islands of the Unalashka District*: 55. "A furious gale with gusts of a hurricane . . ."—*Contributions to the Natural History of Alaska*, Lucien McShane Turner, U.S. Government Printing Office, Washington, D.C., 1886: 48. "The stores are mostly abrupt . . ."—*Descriptive Catalogue of Ethnological Specimens* (manuscript), Natural History Archives, Smithsonian Institution. "This region is the empire of the winds."—Veniaminov, *Notes on the Islands of the Unalashka District*: 53. The prohibition against grumbling about severe weather is also found in Veniaminov's *Notes*, page 276. Alexei Yatchmenef's "Account of a Trip by Baidarka from Sanak Island to Unalaska Village" is found in *Aleut Tales and Narratives*: 304-313. The best account of World War II in the Aleutian Islands is John Haile Cloe's *The Aleutian Warriors*, Part I, Anchorage, Alaska, 1991. Burning crosses for firewood is found in William Draper's "A Brush With War," in *Alaska At War*, edited by Fern Chandonnet, Anchorage, Alaska, 1995.

9. VILLAGE LIVES, VILLAGE GRIEF
"O Sons of Justice! . . ."—*The Hidden Words of Bahá'u'lláh*, translated by Shoghi Effendi, Bahá'í Publishing Trust, Wilmette, Illinois, 1963: 23. "Glorified art Thou . . ."—*Bahá'í Prayers*, Bahá'í Publishing Trust, Wilmette, Illinois, 1967: 22-23.

10. TURNING CORNERS
For information on Russian fur hunters, see Lydia Black's "Promyshlenniki . . . Who Were They?" in *Bering and Chirikov: The American Voyages and Their Impact*,

edited by O.W. Frost, Alaska Historical Society, Anchorage, Alaska, 1992. Aleut hats are pictured and discussed in detail in Lydia Black's *Glory Remembered: Wooden Headgear of Alaska Sea Hunters*, Alaska State Museum, 1991. The letter to the Child Rescue Department is found in the Applegate papers, Alaska Historical Library, Juneau, Alaska. For a sociological study of Unalaska prior to the Alaska Native Claims Settlement Act, see Dorothy M. Jones's *Aleuts in Transition: A Comparison of Two Villages*, University of Washington Press, Seattle, 1976. The story of Agalinax̂ is in *Aleut Tales and Narratives*, 228-231.

11. A SPRING HIKE
Hulten's comment on the weather on May 1, 1932, is in *Flora of the Aleutian Islands*, page 36. For the accounts by Captain James Cook and others in his expedition, see *The Voyage of the "Resolution" and "Discovery" 1776-1780*, edited by J.C. Beaglehole, Cambridge, published for the Hakluyt Society at the University Press, 1967. The story about the downing of the PBY off Egg Island is in Henry Swanson's *The Unknown Islands*, page 161. The Aleut evacuation during World War II has been described by Dean Kohlhoff in *When the Wind Was a River*, University of Washington Press, Seattle, 1995. Additional information on the evacuation and the destruction of houses and churches is in *Personal Justice Denied: Report of the Commission on Wartime Relocation and Internment of Civilians*, Washington, D.C., December 1982, and in *A Sure Foundation: Aleut Churches in World War II*, Barbara Sweetland Smith with Patricia J. Petrivelli, Aleutian/Pribilof Islands Association, Anchorage, Alaska, 1994.

12. VILLAGE LIVES, VILLAGE FRIENDSHIPS
A transcription of Anfesia Shapsnikoff's talk with schoolchildren is found in *Unugulux Tunusangin, Oldtime Stories*.

13. PATTERNS
For help in remembering what Unalaska was like in 1972, I am indebted to a report, May 1972, prepared by the Planning and Zoning Commission of Unalaska under the chairmanship of Richard LaCourse and Roy Tuttle.

14. AN ALTERED LANDSCAPE
Information on the *ikax̂* is found in Veniaminov, *Notes on the Islands of the Unalashka District*, translated by Lydia T. Black and R.H. Geoghegan, The Elmer E. Rasmuson Library Translation Program, University of Alaska, Fairbanks, and The Limestone Press (page 233); Bergsland, *Aleut Dictionary* (page 287); William S. Laughlin, *Aleuts: Survivors of the Bering Land Bridge*, Holt, Rinehart and Winston, 1980 (page 138); Ray Hudson, editor, *Unugulux Tunusangin, Oldtime Stories*, Unalaska City School District, 1992 (pages 160-167); Barbara Sweetland Smith with Patricia J. Petrivelli, *A Sure Foundation: Aleut Churches in World War II*, Aleutian/Pribilof Islands Association, 1994. The accuracy of the 1764 conflict is discussed in Laughlin, *Aleuts: Survivors of the Bering Land Bridge*, page 120-126. For the poems of Theodore Roethke, see his volumes *Words for the Wind* and *Far Field*, Doubleday & Company, Garden City, N.Y. The William Blake quotation is from his long poem, *Milton*.

15. THE FINISHED BASKET
Anfesia Shapsnikoff's exhortations were originally published in Aleut and English in several issues of a local Unalaska newspaper, *The Unalaskan*, and were reprinted in *Unugulux Tunusangin: Oldtime Stories*, Unalaska City School District, Unalaska, Alaska, 1992: 215-217.